LESLIE LEE SANDERS

Ready to Listen?

A SPIRITUAL
SELF-HELP MEMOIR

ISBN: 979-8-9935132-1-8 (eBook)
ISBN: 979-8-9935132-0-1 (Paperback)

Book cover and interior by Damonza.
Edited by Ainsley James.

First printing edition 2025.

LLS Books
Mesa, Arizona, 85212

www.llsanders.com

To my three girls.

To my spirit team.

To me.

Contents

Preface

SPIRIT TOLD ME to write this book, and I listened.

By the time that message came through, I had already lived a lifetime of trauma, success, and forty-three years of spiritual guidance delivered through synchronicities, symbols, dreams, visions, astral projections, angelic visitations, and the kind of insight some might call divine… yet others might dismiss as imagination or make believe.

But imagination has always been my greatest ally. It shaped me as a storyteller, a gift I discovered as a young girl, begging my mother to tell me scary stories whenever I could steal a moment of her undivided attention. That was no easy feat for a single mother in a house bursting with seven daughters and a son.

Looking back, I believe every experience, every hardship, and every skill I've honed led me here, to this book in your hands. Because if there is one thing I know about a life purpose, it's this: when the call comes, you answer.

And here's the thing, these same spiritual tools that guided me are guiding you, too. The Universe is always speaking, always nudging, always offering signs. When you learn to recognize them, interpret them, and align your efforts with their direction, you can manifest anything your heart desires.

Storytellers pass down insight and knowledge by

connecting, engaging, and entertaining through sharing stories. Allow me to share mine. This is the story of how I brought every wish in my life to fruition and how you can too. Part self-help guide. Part Memoir. All true.

Ready to listen?

How to Read this Book

Throughout this book, particular thoughts and insight appears in the text and are specified as such:

The voice of intuition, spirit, (angels, spiritual guides, ancestors, the Universe, source, universal consciousness, higher self, God) or my spiritual team are depicted in bold.

The voice of my rational thinking, logical thoughts, scientific brain, or three-dimensional mind are depicted in italics.

Introduction

I SIT BEFORE MY laptop a half hour before midnight, a leg bouncing up and down under the large wooden desk as I stare at the screen. The house is nearly silent at this hour, except for the latest K-pop music playing mindlessly on the TV.

Every now and then the air conditioner clicks on, rattling the lint-caked filter and disturbing the sense of flow I had.

It's been this way every night for the past few weeks. Along with an intense sense of anxiety and unease at the state of the world. Headlines, real or manufactured, packed with keywords of war, corruption, and human rights violations.

What's a forty-three-year-old Black American woman to do?

You're on the right track.

But am I?

Keep going.

I listen to the guidance and finally words appear on the laptop screen as my fingers quickly graze the

1

keyboard. I'm not quite sure what form the words will take once completed, but I push through my racing thoughts that try to sabotage me.

For months, my mind has been riddled with self-limiting thoughts, fears, and worries, after realizing the truth about my career. Suddenly, I lost all will to create, even though creating is my purpose.

I know what I'm supposed to do. I even know what steps to take to get there. I just can't do it. Something is holding me back.

I just imagine, seeing the visual in my mind's eye: Me as a spiritual warrior, clad in my armor and wielding a double-edged sword. Standing at the front lines of the ultimate battle, alongside millions of spiritual warriors. We're standing on the side of right, good, peace and unity. We're defending our power by shielding the souls who may lack enlightenment.

Although I see the scene as if it was right before my eyes, I still contemplate how to get the images from my head and onto paper. How do I convince you, yes YOU, that you are one of those warriors?

You can just tell them. Tell them how you know. Tell them who you are.

I was given the wisdom to see the truth. The truths of the world and their systems and their control tactics, truths that are hidden behind one's smile or neutrality, and truths in the hearts and intentions in everyone around me. I see the superficial directly but never take it at face value because many wear masks and veneers to either hide their truths or because they haven't discovered it yet. I see the truth in others that lay hidden in the depths of their subconscious, reasons why they treat their significant other the way they do or why they speak so fast it's as if they're trying to vomit up the words. I know when someone's been hurt despite their smile and laughter. I know when someone's done the hurting even when it's hidden behind the act of normalcy.

I'm aware of the power of normalcy. Every society has their own. The pressure to conform, to stay in line, to follow, to copy, to become a group mind, are a part of herd mentality—sheep. And we all participate so we don't become ostracized, kicked out, or othered. We seek acceptance and validation from others because those are measures of how close we are to being accepted as part of a community. This is because we equate acceptance and validation with love and belonging.

We all wear masks. Including me, I wore several masks for forty-three years, my whole life. And only recently I began removing them.

I wore the mask of normalcy. The mask that allows me to blend in with the rest of society. The one everyone in my chosen communities sees to accept me as one of them.

But in writing these words, I'm taking the masks off and revealing my true, authentic self. The version of me that expresses my doubts of a person's character. I no longer stay in relationships that I know are unhealthy even if it all appears fine on the surface. I will not tolerate the false personalities, the veneers, the masks of others, especially if it causes more harm than good.

Living a lie has never done more good than harm.

Chapter 1

Early Glimpses of Spirit

ONE OF THE first times I became aware of the spiritual realm was when I had an out of body experience at around the age of seven.

It was an early night as I lay on Mom's bed in her pitch-black bedroom. The only light came from the digital clock on the nightstand where the display flooded the room in a dim hue of red.

Lying on my back, I stared up at the ceiling, trying to fall asleep while my older sisters and Mom were talking in the living room. A sense of peace washed over me and suddenly I was floating near the ceiling, looking down at my sleeping body in the bed. Confused, I glanced around the room with the help of the glowing red numbers on the clock while a sliver of living room light seeped under the crack of the closed bedroom door.

Is that me?

I focused on the details of what looked like my face and body on the bed as it lay motionless with closed eyes. I was aware of my surroundings, being conscious and alert enough to feel my weightlessness.

That is your body.

The more I tried to make sense of what was happening, the faster I spun to the right several feet over my body. The sensation of being lightweight and floating was apparent as I tried to understand how similar our limbs were. They were both spread apart in the same position. I couldn't rise higher as I sensed an invisible umbilical cord keeping me attached to my physical body.

Suddenly, the conversation Mom was having in the living room with my siblings became clearer, as if I was right there in the room with them. Yet, I continued floating and spinning over my body.

What's happening?

I wasn't scared. In fact, it was highly amusing. Little old me thought it was kind of cool. I couldn't wait to tell my family what I was experiencing. But just as I attempted to further explore, something tugged in my gut. The feeling is similar to the sensation of your stomach dropping right before taking a plunge in a rollercoaster. Next thing I knew, I fell back into my body.

I jolted straight up in bed. Eyelids snapped open to the familiar flood of red from the clock on the nightstand. I glanced down, seeing my physical body from the common angle…the chest down.

I rushed out of bed, ran out of the room and into the living room, interrupting whatever Mom and my sisters were discussing. "I was floating, Mom! I was in bed and then I was floating and saw myself in the bed at the same time."

They laughed. All of them.

"She's in there dreaming, thinking she's floating and stuff." More laughs and head shakes.

From that encounter I learned I couldn't tell them about the weird things I experience. They dismissed it and even ridiculed a profound experience I just had.

Never again.

So later when me and my friends found a cute but dead bird, we buried it in a little patch of dirt near our home and performed a funeral for it. With small purple flowers arranged around the burial site, we held hands and prayed to the angels to take the little birdie to Heaven.

I never told them that I envisioned a tall, feminine angel standing over my right shoulder with wings as beautiful as those of the dead bird. I asked the angel to, "please make sure the birdie gets to Heaven." Later that day, the thought came over us. What if the bird was no longer there? The others may have been driven by curiosity, I was driven by finding proof that the angel I imagined was really there. We gently removed the dirt.

And couldn't find it.

We checked the placements of each flower to make sure they were not disturbed before sifting through the dirt, and even digging further below, to find nothing. Not even a feather. I knew then that angels were real. That they answered our prayers and took the little birdie to Heaven. They satisfied our curiosity and answered my question at the same time, possibly making believers out of my friends too.

But then, being a human with a logical mind, my brain started going to work.

Maybe a wild animal or a stray dog took the bird.

But you checked the flowers and the mound of dirt. It was the exact way you left it.

Yea. But what if someone dug up the bird and put the dirt and flowers back the way we had them to trick us.

Why would someone go through all that trouble just to trick you?

Well, maybe the bird wasn't dead, but we thought it was, and it unburied itself and flew away.

And left the mound intact and the flowers undisturbed?

Yea…that doesn't make any sense.

We never saw the bird again and that memory stayed with me ever since. But my curiosity about angels was now in full effect. Ever since that experience, I became even more curious about these divine beings. Do they really come to help you if you ask them to? Do we all have an angel? Are they even real?

At age eight, I was provided an answer.

Although my younger sister had cerebral palsy after being born with her umbilical cord wrapped around her neck, depriving oxygen to her brain, she was special for surviving the odds. Doctors said she wouldn't make it to the age of ten. She became our family's miracle when she surpassed that to live to thirty-five.

However, my brother was the real special addition to our family, in my eyes. He would often get away with hell because he was the only boy out of seven girls. There were the four oldest who were a tight bunch, and us younger four shared a father, making us a tight bunch. Until he died at age thirty-five too, two years after the miracle sister.

But back then, when my brother was just a baby, he was rushed to the hospital. I was just a kid, a little black girl, so I knew nothing. I didn't know why he needed a hospital or why I was there with Mom and my dad.

I was often with Mom at the doctor's office visits, pretending to not be affected by the swelling and bruising she would try to hide with bandanas—but that's her story to tell.

This time, I was told to sit in the waiting room while Mom went back into the office with my brother and the doctor. Sitting alone in a chair, I tried to be patient, waiting and wondering if I should worry or not.

Then the most out of place child walked into the space, grabbing my attention with her pale skin and unusually long, lustrous curly black hair. I've never seen hair as long and big on a kid. Her appearance reminded me of a real-life doll.

She sat beside me. Her attention had been on me the whole time, so I knew she was coming to speak. "Your brother will be okay. You don't have to worry."

I nodded, feeling awkward, but the unease was normal for me in public spaces.

"His stomach is the issue, but they will be able to fix it, and he will be okay," she went on.

Who is this girl? Does she know me or Mom? Should I know her?

I finally opened my mouth. "How do you know?"

"Because I'm an angel."

I gave her the side eye, expecting to see feathered wings on her back or a golden halo to appear around her head. "You don't look like an angel."

"Angels have many forms. I look this way because it's comfortable for you. I think you should know that your brother will be alright."

She stood and walked toward the nurse's desk as if going on with her other duties. As she walked away, I couldn't take my eyes off her hair, secretly envious of the curls and length. I wondered if her parents were the adult couple near the desk and if she was trying to play a trick on me. But I couldn't get over how she didn't speak like any other kid.

She left the space, and I couldn't wait to tell Mama about the girl with the prettiest hair and what she had to say.

I waited until we got back into the car and were on our way back home. "Mama, a girl came up to me and said she was an angel and that my brother will be okay." I explained the situation with his stomach in detail, using the words she used to describe his condition. "She said it will be fixed."

Mama turned in her seat to look back at me. "How do you know all that?"

"The little girl told me. She had big, pretty hair too. It was so long, it went passed her butt. Did you see her in the waiting room?" I just knew if they saw the girl they would remember her by her hair.

She didn't see the little girl or understand how I could possibly know what had been confirmed about my brother's health. But thank the Universe, the angel was right.

Chapter 2

The Importance of Stories

THERE ARE TWO most important areas of focus in storytelling, the beginning and the end. The beginning is important because it must hook the reader, while a good ending must resonate, stay with them, and encourage them to take action. But just like a pie, the middle might be the best part.

The center of the story is where extraordinary experiences gradually led me to where I am today. In a grateful existence, even though it hasn't always been that way.

Life for me truly began with the scary stories I used to beg mom to tell me. I had to be no bigger than first grade when mom told me about the infamous funeral her childhood town attended, where one by one, the people would approach the small, makeshift wooden crate to witness the shocking sight of the lifeless infant that was described as half bear and half human.

Now how's that for grabbing someone's attention and imagination?

I used to be stuck in my tracks, captivated by her words.

Mom would detail the dark brown fur that covered the entire baby except for the face. She'd explain how the baby had paws with tiny claws instead of hands and feet, and the most shocking detail was the little horns protruding from the front of its tiny skull.

Horror pricked my skin and trickled down my spine, gripping me in its addictive clutch. The fear was fun and safe because a part of me knew the story was made-up. Yet, I couldn't get enough. My imagination soared with scenes and scenarios.

I needed to know more. What did everyone do when they saw what was in the small crate? Who were the parents? How had the final resting place become a halfhearted wooden box?

I couldn't wait to memorize the details so I could pass it on to my friends at school or the kids around the neighborhood. The storyteller I was born to be had been activated, even though I hadn't realized it yet.

What other stories did Mama have in her collection? The scarier tales contained enough detail, witnesses and 'evidence' that made it even more fascinating and easier to believe.

After she shared certain shocking details, I would interrupt, "For real, Mom? Are you lying?"

She'd shake her head convincingly, satisfying my hungry imagination. "For real! Go ask your aunt. She was there with me." By mentioning known witnesses, she made the story even more unsettling, because if my aunt was there, it had to be real.

I'd test her by fishing for more detail, trying to catch her slipping up. "And what did Auntie do when the dance floor split open?"

She didn't even have to think about the answer. "Everyone on the dancefloor backed up against the walls of the club as the crack grew bigger and wider." She'd say with an honest face and vocal inflections to match. "And the music just kept on bumping, and the club lights kept on flashing. And because it happened so fast, not even the DJ knew why everyone was running off the dancefloor. When I focused, I realized a big hole had opened in the middle of the dancefloor," she'd spread her arms wide for emphasis, "and we were staring down into it."

"What was down there?" My eyes grew big, and my imagination conjured up endless possibilities. Which creepy direction could this story go?

"Finally, the music stopped and while everyone's attention was on the deep, dark abyss, a giant red skinned devil crawled up from the hole."

I narrowed my eyes. That seemed a little farfetched for my liking, and suddenly it became hard for me to suspend my disbelief like I desperately wanted to. I smacked my lips. "You're lying." I tried to dismiss her.

"No, no." She'd shake her head. "I'm telling you, go ask your aunt. She'll tell you exactly what I just said. The man was as big as the ceiling, and he crawled out of the hole looking around at all of us. Judging us."

"What did he look like?" I said, giving her a chance to convince me that the events really did happen.

"He had blood red skin and big black horns on his head, and sharp claws at the ends of his fingers," she went on. "His voice was deep when he growled."

The visuals were enough to keep me entertained and occupied, but I wanted more. "And what did you and Auntie do?"

"We ran out the front door and took ourselves home. We're never going back there again."

And that marked the end of the story of the Devil in the Nightclub. In fact, anything that happened after the story sessions wasn't important. All the scares were over. Yet, I'd always ask for another story, and she'd somehow come up with more spooky supernatural events. Just how many ghosts, devils, and demon babies can one person encounter in a lifetime and live to talk about it?

It was a lot to take in and would have my mind pondering for hours, but in a good way. Building up my interest in stories with twisted endings or unpredictable revelations. Little did I know, most of her stories reflected her mindset at the time and what was preached to her through the church and society.

Back then, being young and impressionable, parables or Bible stories with messages and lessons for humanity were also some of my favorite stories. Adam and Eve, Noah's Ark, Moses and the Red Sea, King Solomon, David and Goliath, Samson and Delila, the Book of Job, and The Book of Revelations were the most memorable.

They were told in a similar fashion to how Mama told her stories, as if they were real events that took place instead of tales written to understand a moral lesson about yourself and humanity.

But being fascinated with storytelling, I quickly learned that there was wisdom in any story, be it real or make believe.

The stories Mama told me, like that of the human teddy bear, were warnings about being caught up in other people's business and how being nosy could backfire on you. Her story about the devil at the nightclub was a warning about the dangers of getting involved in dangerous situations in places you didn't belong.

Like fairytales, Bible legends, and Mama's tales, the story of my life may seem farfetched. But unlike those tales, my story is real.

Everything that happened in our pasts led us where we are today, and we could use those lessons to create the life we want now and in the future.

There are lessons to learn in every story if you care to listen, insight to gain from all stories if you care to interpret, and advice to gather from any story if you care to apply what you learn from them.

Even at such a young age, I didn't realize how much stories would play a huge role in my life. I would go on to seek out similar short stories and fairytales. The first stories I was introduced to early as a child were the short, memorable nursery rhymes like Mary and her little lamb.

I enjoyed the fables I read in school. My teachers would show us how to think critically about a story by reading short tales of folklore and asking us to identify the moral or message of the story.

What is the message the author is trying to get across in this tale? What message is the Universe trying to convey in our lives?

Teachers would explain how the characters, plot, and events all had a reason to be there other than the surface journey that took place. In every story there is subtext, the deeper message, a lesson to learn.

Little did Mama know, I had my own stories to tell. Real life encounters about astral projection, or out-of-body experiences, angel visitations, and communication with Spirit all before the age of five, and long before Mama's first story left her mouth.

So, I wonder. Are *you* ready to listen?

Chapter 3

The Power of the Voice

OR A LONG time, I wasn't ready to listen to the nudging of the Universe. I didn't have a voice. I never had a voice. Whenever I spoke, it was immediately met with a, "Sit down and be quiet," especially in my childhood. Those times where I spoke anyway, my words would be ignored. What did I know? I was just a little black girl with no knowledge of how the world worked, so why would anyone consider what I had to say?

That was the message the world tried to convey to me, but little did everyone know, I knew quite a lot. I was aware of many truths even at a young age. I understood right from wrong, good from bad, and that innate ethical and moral compass led me to become the best version of myself.

I had an urgent need to provide and seek equality, justice, compassion and honesty in my life. I knew this way of living would lead to a fulfilling existence. I lived by the belief what you put out in the world comes back to you, in more ways than one. Therefore, I treated everyone the way I liked to be treated.

Unfortunately, I failed to realize that not everyone followed an ethical or moral compass. By the time I realized that, it was too late.

When I witnessed people hurting or mistreating others for personal gain, it troubled me. The act of even knowing that someone was hurt stayed with me for days, even now. Hearing stories of women or children being harmed will stay in my mind for weeks. I would imagine their pain and fear, and I felt the agony. Only recently did I realize this is the result of having empathy.

The act of placing yourself in someone else's situation to feel what they're feeling. This is the reason I stopped reading and watching the news, it physically, emotionally and mentally distresses me seeing so much injustice, pain and suffering. It became difficult to forgive or forget the pain others caused.

It wasn't the occasional bitchiness, petty fights, nasty arguments, little white lies, or misunderstandings that struck me so deep. It was the surprise of seeing a person's true character and their inability to learn from their past or mistakes.

Evil exists in this world and sometimes it bothers me that I'm forced to live alongside it on this planet.

Every person on Earth has the capacity to be a good human being. However, some choose to give the steering wheel to their misery.

I could sense other's intentions in their demeanor, facial expressions, body language, but mainly from their energy. Because sometimes what appears to be genuine is a mask to hide true feelings. So, I read their vibes, the energy of their intentions, and not rely on just their actions or words.

Still, speaking my truth was rare, especially when my words would often be dismissed. Because who gave *me* the authority to judge another human being?

That's how the power of storytelling took centerstage in my life. I would scribble down my short little horror stories, hoping the plot twists or surprise endings would captivate others. Maybe then they would pay attention to my words.

In church, I heard, "sit still and be quiet." In school, they'd tell me to, "only speak when spoken to." At home, a rule was to, "never butt in when grown folks are speaking."

Even as we struggled alongside other low-income families in the Projects, I would sometimes manage to survive on scraps of food if not one serving from the big family meal of the day.

Asking our neighbors for hotdogs or packs of processed sandwich meat was just as normal as asking to borrow an egg or a cup of sugar. Shame doesn't exist for hungry children, especially when the community shares the struggle. Even now looking back, I understand we had to do what was necessary to survive.

One time, I got to school too late for lunch. Not having any food all day, I told the front office I was hungry, hoping they would allow me to grab a tray from the cafeteria before heading to class. Instead, they handed me a pack of saltine crackers with two inside to satiate me. Were they not trained to spot the signs of a starving child?

The irony is I looked up to teachers so much. As a kid, when others would ask what I wanted to be when I grew up, allowing the word *teacher* to escape my lips was natural. Out of all the jobs available for kids to choose from—a cop, an astronaut, a firefighter, a doctor—my sights were set on teaching important lessons for growth.

I kept that desire to teach until the sixth grade. At eleven years old, I discovered something that would change the direction of my life forever. During our weekly trip to the library, my favorite hour of the week, I discovered the book *Scary Stories to Tell in the Dark*.

My jaw dropped as my sights set on the eerie book cover, and even more so as I skimmed the words and images throughout the collection of short scary stories for young adults. A familiar warmth swelled my heart as it took me back to Mama's short, creepy tales. I immediately imagined my name on the book cover instead. That's when I knew, being an author was my calling.

I should have known. During reading time in class, I loved nothing more than sitting on the floor with the rest of the kids, surrounding the teacher in the chair as she read a variety of children-friendly books out loud.

English became my favorite subject in school as I got to read and write stories as assignments. Writing became a huge hobby in my free time as I made up short scary stories to try to mimic the book that had inspired me. I wouldn't go anywhere without my notebook. Choosing to sit in the back of the school bus alone for privacy as I wrote and drew illustrations for the monsters I created.

My characters and plots got a few unintended laughs from some or criticism from others, but this was preparing me for real world critique, feedback, and rejection that is a staple in the publishing industry.

These moments were preparing me. Every experience in

life, especially when it involved creativity, taught me important lessons that equipped me for what was to come.

My inner power, my spirit, was urging me on this path but allowing me to grow and learn along the way. To strengthen me, push me to do better, and sometimes even test my ambition. It wasn't just the sting of the kids' mean comments. It was the Universe testing my will.

Was I ready for this journey? Did I have what it takes to push myself through adversity? Did I really want this?

It was hard to keep the fire to write alive, especially then, but that's how determined I was to see my dream of having my name on a book cover come true. To have my voice finally heard.

Chapter 4

The Masks We Wear

AS MUCH AS I wanted to become a published author, I needed to understand who I really was. Like everyone else, I was playing a part, putting on a mask, and refusing to allow my authenticity to shine.

I always felt like such an outsider, trying to be "normal" like everyone else, trying not to stand out and be noticed for my awkwardness. The worst thing you can do in a conformed society is to be different. Which is why I feared large social gatherings but forced myself to play the "life of the party" even though I knew deep down I was a wallflower.

To understand how being authentic allows us to create the life we want, we first must understand who we are as a spirit having a human experience.

Welcome to Earth School.

Earth is one of the most prestigious, respected, and feared schools from our soul's perspective.

What do I mean by that?

Before our spirit comes into physical, human form, we as spirits in the spiritual realm decide what lessons to undertake with help from our spirit guides or mentors and teachers, to gain the highest degree of all ... enlightenment, awakening or ultimate knowledge.

Once we decide to have a human life, as a spirit we work with our guides to go over the curriculum. What lessons do we need to learn as a human being that can enlighten and grow our spiritual being?

Our spirit guides are needed because Earth is one of the most difficult schools a spirit can choose to learn from. Earth works on the three-dimensional realm, where there are universal laws that we all must follow. On Earth, division exists in every form from the smallest of cells to the largest of the cosmos. The ultimate test of Earth is to balance opposing forces and learn as a human species to live in peace and harmony.

But division, polarities and dualities are strong on Earth. The most charitable, loving, honest person has a counterpart that exists alongside her. Every good natured, compassionate soul must live and thrive alongside some of the evilest hearted and dangerous people. This is what makes Earth so feared, and only those who have the courage and determination choose to come here and take on the challenge.

Like walking blind into an unexplored abyss, it takes a special kind of strength and bravery to face what resides in the darkness, but we come trusting we'll make our way through.

Our souls are born into human bodies and our memory as a spirit disappears because our spirit resides in a higher realm than the 3D. The laws of Spirit are totally different from the laws of the three-dimensional realm where we and Earth reside. This is why science has difficulty discovering spirit. Science relies on 3D tools to try to measure a much higher realm's existence.

We as humans perceive the 3D world with our 5 senses, which are very limited. For example, cats can see in the dark, bats can hear at higher frequencies, and sea creatures are attuned with Earth's magnetic fields, etc.

Our spirit guides remain with us throughout our human lives. They speak to us, guide us, and co-create with us from the spiritual realm, and those who become awakened or aware through self-reflection, introspection or going inward will see this truth.

Once we open our eyes to the existence of our spirit and the spiritual teams that guide us, we've awakened. The more awake we are, the faster the path to enlightenment, where we will not only communicate with spirit, but interpret their guidance.

We tap into this higher realm through intuition, our sixth sense.

How often do we connect with our creative muse to pull inspiration and ideas from a nonphysical space to transform it into a physical, tangible creation for others to enjoy? Like this very book, conceptualized from a thought and transformed into a tool. We have the power to create something from nothing. A mere fantasy, goal or plan can become reality, including a prosperous, abundant, and fulfilling life.

Being authentic is the first step to opening ourselves to the spirit within us, our higher self. That spirit holds all the power we need to make our lives the way we see fit. That spirit remembers the plan that was created on the other side, the curriculum or blueprint, and views it from a higher perspective to guide us through every test we face as a human. That immense power inside of us is enough to change the world.

For a long time, I struggled in my human body, going through my human life, learning my human lessons. Pretending to be someone I wasn't, or silencing my voice, just to fit in. Yet, my higher self, along with my spiritual guides were nudging me the entire time. Giving me signs and synchronicities to remind me of my power and my path especially when I trailed off track.

And now I've learned to communicate to ask for guidance and listen for the answers. I would consult my guides about the direction of my life, and like a tutor they would lead me. I just had to be aware of their answers.

Most of the time, they don't flat out tell me what to do. They speak the language of spirit. I look for their communication in signs, symbols and synchronicities.

At times it feels like I'm straddling a fence as I live my human life while fully trusting the guidance from my spirit side. The very definition of a Medium. Someone who can bridge the physical with the spiritual, see and exist in both realms at once. To tap into the spiritual realm as a human in 3D space.

This gift comes from the maternal side of my family and has been passed down through the generations.

Mama would tell me how as a kid she knew things about people and their lives that she shouldn't have known. After others got scared of her abilities, she hid them away, keeping them to herself. Too afraid to live her authentic truth.

I'm sure my own girls have unusual spiritual gifts, talents, and abilities beyond the occasional reading tarot. When they're ready to discover their inner power, they will find it too.

That's the thing. We must be ready and willing to open the gateway. The Universe is knocking on our door, asking for permission to work with us. We first have to acknowledge the nudge and accept the invitation.

When we see repeated numbers like 1111 on our grocery receipt, on a car's license plate, or in the phone number of a new friend, these are not coincidences. They are introductions from the Universe. Spirit is saying, "Hello. Do you see me? Are you ready to work together? Can we help you build the life you desire?"

Being able to walk between two worlds, the physical and spiritual, doesn't come without its hardships. Like I said, we're human beings on the planet Earth having a three-dimensional experience, which includes logic, reason, and practical, real-world identity. My need to understand things rationally meant I fluctuated back and forth on what I believed to be true, real, possible and provable. But I was also curious about the unseen, the ethereal, the mystical, the spiritual.

As I touched on earlier, as kids, we're born into family, community, and society with strict rules and norms. We're indoctrinated into whatever the adults and people around us teach us and claim is fact. This is true on every level where systems are involved.

My family and surrounding community taught me that the words of the Holy Bible were true, and that Jesus was real. To question this made you an outsider. Later in life, I had many questions. Because those "facts" held a lot of contradictions. Like, if Jesus was born in the Middle East why is he depicted as a blond haired, blue eyed, white man and his disciples had names like John, Peter, and Paul? If Jesus spread love, acceptance and tolerance for all, why does the church not accept people from the LGBTQ community? Why did the Mormon church exclude Black men from priesthood ordination until 1978? Why did many Catholic priests harm children and why was it covered up for so long?

This eventually led me away from organized religion with structured systems of beliefs and practices, and toward spirituality with a personal and individual connection to a greater source.

I was always curious, looking for answers and facts even on the smallest insects like the ant, capturing them in jars with sand and studying how they operated. Or tadpoles I'd collect and care for until I released them when they grew legs. I'd often sit on the back of the couch and stare in the corner of the window at a spider as it trapped flies in its web and spin them in their silk to feed. Fascinated, I would watch these creatures for hours.

Curious about nature, I collected rocks and the shiny glitter-like minerals in sand my teacher called mica. She wondered why during recess I would pick the shiny silver bits out of the dirt. I was a sponge for knowledge. Even trees were fascinating, their leaves unique to each species. I would try to collect leaves too, taping them inside a notebook along with my notes. Life was filled with unknowns that I needed to know to understand my place as a human on Earth.

If that was considered normal kid behavior, imagine how weird it got when I added my deep fascination of the metaphysical to the mix. But I was just as captivated with the mystical, paranormal and supernatural.

Were spirits real? Did we have the ability to communicate with them?

I would spend days in the public library, reading books about ESP or extrasensory perception and how some people claim to have strange abilities to use their mind to move objects with telekinesis, or read thoughts with telepathy. I even learned that the United States government hired remote viewers to try and look behind enemy lines with only their minds and how accurate their descriptions and drawings were.

Extraordinary people with strange abilities were out there. So, maybe the unexplained phenomenon I experienced wasn't so farfetched.

Magic, spells, and seances became a fun, innocent pastime for me and my younger siblings and cousins to partake in. Our sessions would usually start with me telling spooky stories that escalated into us becoming the characters in our own eerie tales when something bizarre would happen.

And the bizarre would often occur.

Throughout my life, I straddled the line between real and imagined, practical and artistic, grounded and in the clouds. I used to think I needed to be one or the other, labeling myself strange if I wavered between the two.

I've come to learn that it is a gift.

My empathy allowed me to understand the human experience enough to know the hidden truth about the people I encounter. The town's drunk is not only a person who refuses to get their life together and decides to escape reality through alcohol until they drink their life away. Empathy allows me to figurately step into their shoes and see the full picture, not just the one degree they show to the world. I see them struggle with the pressure to be a perfect parent and spouse without credit for busting their ass for twelve hours a day, seven days a week and needing time off and better pay. I see their need for a break or breakthrough.

Empathy is the link to our power and spirit. We need to feel and understand our feelings to connect with Spirit and other humans on a spiritual level.

Society pushes down our power by making us believe feeling emotions other than anger is a weakness. Therefore, having feelings—which is a human experience—suddenly becomes undesirable. They make us believe a strong Black female can't be emotional or upset or else we're labeled "aggressive" or fall into the "angry Black woman" stereotype. They tell men that being masculine means getting rid of the tears. "Don't cry, don't care, don't feel."

This programming and conditioning are other ways to diminish our power. Without power, we're forced to accept unfair laws, flawed ideologies, beliefs, and their bullshit. We accept their unfair treatment, shitty wages, and blatant hate because they successfully transformed us from wolves to sheep.

Wolves are lone creatures, following their instinct and oftentimes leading the pack. They're vicious and dangerous only when need be. Sheep follow the crowd, they keep their head down and do what the shepherd instructs them to do, even if it harms themselves or others. And sheep don't realize they're being led to the cliffs, they blindly trust, without question.

The only people who enjoy labels, boxes, and conformity are those at the top creating the rules, laws, and systems that construct those traps. This is why we're told to respect authority figures even when they do harm, because many people are falsely led to believe those in power can do no harm or the harm that's done is for the purpose of the greater good.

Police officers are meant to protect, so even when they unjustly kill, we're led to believe it was out of protection. Religious leaders are meant to guide, so when they do harm, we're led to believe they were a bad apple from the bunch. Elected leaders are meant to represent us and our needs as citizens, so when they become corrupt and turn against our interest, we're led to believe the facts are fake news.

Strip us of our power and we become blinded, aimless sheep. We no longer think critically or deeply, or understand the people, experiences, and the world around us. We repeat what we see and hear from other sheep and that has become the norm.

But we are so much more than that, and it's time we wake up to that fact.

Discover our power, our spirit within.

That's when we can begin to see how systems trained us to go along with the bullshit. How we were born into thinking and believing certain things because those around us did. We keep tradition without asking why it exists in the first place, mindlessly doing what those before us did.

I started doing the thinking and analyzing myself, but to get to that point, I had to go inside and figure out who I was, asking myself honest questions and uncovering the truth no matter how painful. I became completely transparent with myself.

Who was I? What did I want out of life? Why do I exist in this world? Why me?

Those answers led to more questions. Why do I believe the

things I believe? Did I really trust certain information or was I taking on someone else's opinions? Why does it matter to me?

This is how I became aware of the masks we wear and when I began taking them off. This is how I awakened to my power within, finally realizing it exists, and understanding how it works. But to toss the masks, I first had to meet the authentic me. And for that to happen, I needed to go within.

Solitude allows us to sit with the chaos of our mind, ask questions about our true wants and wishes and uncover the whys. This is the time to figure out what makes us who we are when we're not in the public eye. This is the time to be real with ourselves. What makes us happy? What about us needs change, growth or adjustment? Confront what prevents us from being our true selves due to embarrassment, fear or discomfort while in the safety of our thoughts.

Start showing up as that person, little by little, as the layers are peeled back over time.

My process began with me being unaware, not even realizing I had fabricated the masks. I'm sure it's similar for most. Only recently, since I had the most life changing experience, I realized I was becoming my true, authentic self.

The Arizonan girl who enjoyed singing random songs out of nowhere. Who thinks adding a random cussword to the end of every line of a popular song for emphasis is hilarious. The girl who loves K-pop, 90s Pop music and the greatest five-part harmony boyband that ever existed. The girl who lives and breathes horror movies, scary stories and analyzes their hidden messages or commentary. The girl who made friends with a crow and named him Crow Buddy (but has yet to confirm the bird's gender), enjoys wild animals, mountains, talking to plants and trees, and enjoying all of Earth's life and wonders.

On a surface level, that's who I really am behind the scenes. Why would I ever mask those things?

Society, that's why. Our society says we can't be too weird or unique because we would upset the status quo. At least that's the consensus. That's how we function. Blend in or become an outcast. So many of us rather place on a mask to become part of the greater whole instead of showcasing or expressing our individuality.

This mindset keeps us stuck. It keeps us right where we're at—where everyone else wants us to be.

And I'm done with that.

Aren't you? Yes, YOU.

So, stripping away the masks requires change.

This process can take time, years or decades even, but once we finally know who we truly are and what we stand for, we become authentic. And from that moment on, we'll refuse to wear a mask ever again.

It's a conscious decision to remove a part of our false identity and exchange it with our truth.

Because only two months ago since writing these very words, I walked away from a decent career in writing. I was at a place where I was finally making money writing fiction on a well-known online platform. After two years of continuing to bust my ass, I realized I had been taken advantage of. I wasn't getting paid what I should have for the work I was doing. The betrayal took a chunk of my power away.

I struggled to fulfill my contract and get the last few words on the page, losing my passion for creating characters and worlds along the way. The love of writing quickly became a hatred, and I just wanted out. Months of pushing myself, sitting at the computer every day to get any words down. Until I finished it.

I was finally free.

Still my passion to write was nowhere to be found. Mentally, I quit before the story was even complete. The lack of reciprocity stifled me.

Writing and creating was what I was put on this Earth to do. I knew as a little kid after realizing writing and storytelling was my dream. I knew I'd see my name on books, in libraries and bookstores, and that people would know my name.

There was no doubt. Even then as an eleven-year-old sixth grader, my destiny was to be a well-respected author. Because following guidance from our Spirit will never lead us astray. It's happened to me time and time again.

So how did I get stuck if I was already on a path to embracing who I was? The answer? Giving away my power.

As a writer, one of my biggest goals was to have my book made into a movie. That seemed to be the ultimate way to measure success in the publishing world. Beyond being published, having your book adapted to film or TV was the pinnacle of success. At that point, you made it to the top.

Would you believe the writer that could manifest the life she wants if that writer managed to get her story pitched to Hollywood execs, sat in several calls with powerful people with connections, discussing how to make a visual adaptation happen?

Because that was me. I was right there, in the talks, making my dreams happen, but everything fell through. Something told me that company wasn't right for me, but I didn't listen.

However, if I got there once, I could do it again and succeed. It's destiny, part of my blueprint.

I helped create the life I wanted. I manifested my amazing husband, family, and career and all the accomplishments I had in between. I made my wishes come true. And we all have that ability.

I was always reminded of my power, of that spirit from a higher realm that resided within, of the team of spiritual guides that supported me throughout life. That spiritual team knew the path I planned to take when we were working on my life's blueprint, and they pop in now and then to remind me that I'm capable of creating my dream life as a human as well.

We all are!

How do I prove I'm an authority on this topic? How do I prove what I'm saying is true?

My guides and higher self reminds me I don't need to prove myself to anyone. This is what I'm working on as we speak.

Don't prove. Just be.

Chapter 5

The Language of Spirit

THE UNIVERSE SPEAKS to us in its own language using signs, symbols and synchronicities.

The physical and spiritual realms each have their own sets of laws that keep them separate. Since the Universe, spirit guides and our higher self are spiritual beings in the spiritual realm, the universal laws we measure using our three-dimensional methods prevent their messages from manifesting easily in our physical world. For science to accurately measure spiritual presence it requires the proper spiritual tools.

One of the best ways for Spirit to communicate with us is through our intuition. This is the same space our inspiration, ideas, and imagination exist in. Even though we're capable, not everyone connects with their intuition, so Spirit uses physical methods like signs, symbols and synchronicities in the physical world to communicate. It's like tapping in from the spiritual realm through the telephone to connect to us in the physical realm in a phone call.

According to Google, "A phone works by converting your voice or data into a digital signal that is transmitted as radio waves to a cell tower, which then routes the signal through a network of towers and switching centers to the intended recipient. The recipient's phone receives these radio waves, converts them back into a digital signal, and then into sound or data that the user can understand. This process allows for two-way communication via a decentralized "cellular" network, enabling calls and data to be sent and received over long distances."

To understand how Spirit communicates with us from their realm, they must convert their voice and data into physical signs, symbols, and synchronicities that the recipient must interpret to understand the communication.

Signs from Spirit are like a billboard containing a blatant message. For example, if a butterfly lands on the door of your dream house and you're contemplating a move. That's a sign.

Symbols are objects and images that represent something other than its original meaning. For instance, butterflies are insects, but they also represent change or transformation.

Synchronicities are meaningful coincidences. Not only a chance encounter, like looking up just as a shooting star crosses the night sky. Synchronicities have meaning, like thinking how rare seeing a shooting star is before looking up at the sky to catch one. It's more meaningful because of the timing.

However, the main language of Spirit is intuition.

Intuition is a feeling, a knowing sensation usually in our heart or gut. When Spirit warns us of danger or gives a heads-up, we usually feel it deep in our stomach. Like a gut punch but from the inside. It's a similar sinking feeling that happens when we're on the downward drop of a rollercoaster.

Nudges and positive confirmation are usually felt in the heart, like when choosing a new home and our heartbeat catches and our hearts ache for a second before adrenaline triggers our excitement centers. The heart is the connection to your higher self, the spiritual version of us.

Another form of communication is through channeling. Channeled messages are not just our intuition giving us nudges but translating words or messages from Spirit directly.

The first time I discovered channeling was years ago while writing erotic romance in my earlier years as a professional author. Sure, read that again. At the time I questioned a weird phenomenon that would happen to me during my writing sessions.

I became immersed in the zone becoming so deeply enthralled in what I was writing, describing the scenes in my head so readers could envision the characters and the world. It was only after I measured my progress that I realized I couldn't remember what I had just written. I would reread the text I had just typed down and be utterly surprised and excited by what came out of my mind and onto the page.

Ooh, that's a good line. I wrote that?

I would edit my work and blush at what was written, not remembering it all came from me. Or did it?

Even to this day, I will reread one of my published works and be surprised by the writing, twists and turns, the plot, and sometimes huge passages as most of the intricate details of the story were forgotten. I self-consciously believed my writing

41

was utter shit and my nonexistent professional experience contributed to my lack of success, until I approached it as a stranger.

It was as if I was totally disconnected from my stories while I'm writing them.

The more profound time I realized I was channeling directly from Spirit as recently as me writing these words. During one of my many self-care sessions, I'd bathe for at least an hour where I'd rest my mind and mediate. I suddenly was hit with an abundance of ideas and thoughts that I tried to write them down in the notepad of my phone, but it took too long to get it all written down. So, I began recording a voice memo and my bathtime sessions changed.

Suddenly, I allowed my thoughts and ideas to flow out of my mouth without much thought. It was like lending my physical vessel to my higher self. So much information and ideas about intuition and what it is and how it works flowed from my lips. It felt like the words needed to come out, not from me but from something much more knowledgeable and powerful.

So, I leant my voice to Spirit as an instrument. The following words are from that channeled message.

CHANNELED MESSAGE ABOUT INTUITION JUST FOR YOU

Intuition is that nudge, that urge, that pull, that tug you get in your chest and in your heart that tells you when you need to make a change. It's that tug you feel. It's not butterflies, it's deeper than your gut. It's deeper than anything physical but you feel it. That's your heart. And when you follow your heart, you will find the truth. And not only will you find truth, but it will also lead you down the path of least resistance toward your goals and your purpose.

It tries to lead you down a path that is meant for you so you can encounter what you need to help you grow. So, by the time you make it to your goal you'll be able to hone it, own, claim it and hold on to it. Appreciate it once you get there because you followed your heart and sometimes that path includes a lot of obstacles, pain and setbacks, but all this is to make you aware of certain things, issues, situations, to help you see the truth in the matter. To help you grow stronger in an ability or talent. To push you to keep your determination and motivation strong. To build you into the person you need to be to get you to the next step, and then the next, and each step will continue.

Some will lead you down easier paths because that is what's needed at that time, a quicker path to get you closer to your goals. And some of these paths will lead you to obstacles and lessons you must learn, because once you ace that test, you're now smarter, aware and able to take on the next big thing. And by the time you make it all the way to your goal, wish, dream, you'll have everything you need to fully appreciate it and live in it, fulfilled and full of gratitude. Allow it to sink in that you co-created with the Universe and all that hard work led you there.

The more enlightened you become, the more keys

you have. The more you become the architect of your life. And it's simple, enlightenment is not a woo-woo concept. Enlightenment is being open, authentic and honest with yourself at the least. And those steps to get to that place starts with you going within.

It starts with introspection because the more you learn about yourself, the more layers you unravel and peel away and shatter, the more you're growing and molding into the person you were meant to be on this earth. That person that can now align and move down that path toward that goal, that dream, that wish.

And the truer you are to yourself, the more you sit in authenticity, and the more enlightened you become. Enlightenment means becoming fully aware of what's going on around you, within you, and with others. You're more aware and that brings you closer to understanding people, to understanding everyone, to digging deeper within their roots to see who they truly are. And then you fully immerse yourself in compassion for their struggles and pain. You fully immerse yourself in empathy because you put yourself in their shoes and dig even deeper to discover who they truly authentically are.

All this is enlightenment. It is knowing. The more enlightened you are the more you're able to become the architect of your life. You see that the world has a veneer. You see that the leaders of societies and countries have a veneer. You see that their supporters have veneers. And you see the truth in everyone, realizing that they put on a veneer because they're not comfortable showcasing who they really are. They're afraid of being shamed, judged, ostracized and ultimately unloved and forgotten. That fear makes them put on this facade. You will recognize it and understand the truth in everyone.

And now you can even see the inner workings of everything and why systems are formed, and people follow those systems, rules and laws. And you will see the root of those as well, what causes those, where they're leading to, and what they were made for and why. And you'd be able to influence your world so those things could create what you want in your life.

You just rearrange, switch things, change things, do things differently. You now know what steps you need to take to get closer to those goals. Every time you manifest or create, it becomes a bit easier but will always be difficult because these steps require a lot of dedication and hard work.

Anything worth doing right will not be easy. If it's too easy, you're not doing it right.

END OF CHANNELED MESSAGE

Lately I've been getting messages about being authentic and how important being authentic will benefit me in the years to come, especially the next twenty years while the dwarf planet Pluto is in my zodiac sign of Aquarius.

Just like I mentioned in the preface of this book, my TV talks to me in the most non-Poltergeist kind of way. Through the words others say onscreen, it answers any questions I have.

Mundane questions like, "What's the difference between a river and stream?" To the most profound, "What is my life's purpose and how do I fulfill it?"

While watching online videos, those answers would come. And every time it happened, my heart would drop, and I would recognize it. If I'm watching a video of someone cleaning the rain gutters, unexpectedly I would casually get my answers.

"We want to clear the gutters, otherwise it will back up and flow into the river. Because this here leads to the river that will spread to other counties, even though it looks like a stream. A stream just leads to rivers," they would confirm on TV.

The answers have yet to come to me in strange angelic voices through the TV speaker like, "Leslie, you have been summoned…" Because that's the thing with Spirit and intuition, they work through the 3D laws of our physical world more often than not.

Chapter 6

Failures and Mistakes

A s PART OF the human experience, we all must eat, sleep and shit.

As humans most of us experience negative situations like betrayal, loneliness, pain, and loss along with the positives. We gain knowledge from knowing how it feels to be alone, to be judged, to lose as well as the opposite. Because of our free will, we navigate a 3D world of dualities, polarization and opposites because we're choosing what to learn and apply with each experience.

Failure, rejection and obstacles are important because we learn from those experiences and that's what shapes us into who we are.

Our adolescent years are the perfect time to learn from our mistakes, because this is where we make many of them. This is why I refrain from judging a person's integrity or character for what they've done during this time of their life. Until we become mature minded adults, we're still trying to figure out who we are and what we believe. And the conclusions we come to will change and develop over time.

The young adult years are when we learn our actions have consequences, right from wrong, respect, empathy and compassion, and other important life lessons. Once we become mature minded adults, it's up to us to put those lessons to practice. By then we should have *some* idea of the kind of person we are and who we want to be. We should have some clue what we won't stand for and what we stand with, our ethics, morals and values.

Once we know better. Do better. That's how we grow.

We're required to know physical, emotional, mental, and spiritual unease along with joy, pleasure, and bliss. We're meant to explore these parts of us and use them to improve ourselves and our lives.

As humans, we have the right to make mistakes. In fact, we *will* make mistakes. It's what we do about those mistakes that matter.

Do we blame others for our errors, our childhood upbringing, our parents, our partner, society? Or do we take accountability for our role, and be honest and admit where we could have made better decisions, and learn to not make that mistake again?

The dualities of life—the good and bad, the right and wrong, the truth and lies, the dark and the light—is the design of this Earth school experience. Navigating life through the ups and downs while striving for goals and accomplishments, and meeting failures and opposition gives us multiple chances to better ourselves, grow, learn, change, and evolve. Eventually, humanity grows on a larger scale, creating a true utopia instead of the false utopia the greedy players in power try to make us believe we already got.

Duality, or opposition, is part of the laws of planet Earth. Before we incarnated on Earth as humans, we were souls in the spiritual realm. We worked with our spiritual guides, mentors, and advisors on the other side to navigate Earth school—the most prestigious and renown school in the spiritual realm.

The main reason Earth school is so renowned is because it's difficult and requires the strength of a highly enlightened spirit to acquire a "degree." Why? Because of Earth's duality, the human experiences can range from pure bliss to severely agonizing, and everything in between, all the time.

It's not until later in humanity's timeline that most experiences on Earth sway to the beneficial side of the spectrum instead of hanging around the center and teetering between good and bad. The more enlightened the spirit within the human experience, the closer we get to bringing all sides together to unite in harmony.

CHANNELED MESSAGE ABOUT SELLING YOUR SOUL JUST FOR YOU

Do you want to know what it really means to "sell your soul?" A lot of people believe it's as simple as agreeing to go against your values to have your wishes granted or being willing to damn your soul to Hell to get what you want. And sometimes they think it comes in the form of a contract, like in the entertainment business where you sign shady deals, or becoming a sellout, putting money in the top dog's pockets in the pursuit of fame, power or success.

One thing I've come to learn is how Karma truly works. Although we have free will to put out positivity or negativity or to do "good" or "bad," the balance is that as a spirit being, our Higher Self experiences every human experience we go through from the point of view of each person involved in all our human encounters. Therefore, we could better understand how our actions and decisions truly affect others.

We feel what we put out to others through our five senses, the good and the bad.

When our human lives are over, we return to our higher self in the spiritual realm. Like being born on Earth, we are reborn into spirit. Because a human lifetime is usually lengthy, upon returning to our spiritual form we must be reminded of who we are as a spirit and what we set out to accomplish as a human.

Our guides and passed loved ones meet us upon transition to help us become refamiliarized with our spirit form. And during this process, we are given a life review. We review every event of our human lives from birth to death and are shown how we impacted Earth and its occupants.

And no one judges. Not our guides, passed loved ones, or even ourselves.

We evaluate and feel each experience including how our decisions, words, thoughts, acts and intentions impacted and affected others. During the review, the only "judgment" comes from us in seeing and understanding how we affected others. We become immersed in the life review, seeing the situation from a higher perspective, hearing the thoughts of those involved in specific experiences, feeling their emotions and every physical sensation, while seeing the ripple effects of how we affect their future.

And because time isn't measured the same in the spiritual realm, as spirits we review our entire human lifetime immediately, yet we understand and feel every-single-thing. The entire process is like going over the answers to our completed final exam with our instructor and mentors, fully understanding our life as a human.

We feel every emotional, mental, and physical sensation we cause in others. The pain of every harsh word, the terror of every threat, the agonizing sting of each whack from a belt or switch.

Not only will we review our entire human lifetime to gain more clarity of the lessons we learned, but we also experience the result of our impact on Earth's environment, its inhabitants, and our spirit.

And for those who chose to relish in or promote cruelty, a life review may seem far more tormenting than any manmade Hell.

Yet, when we decide to put good into the world, we experience that too. Every person who was moved by our smile or words of encouragement, we will feel their heart skip a beat and their hope return to them. Each good deed, uplifting word, good intention, etc., will be felt. Even if it's unintentional, we will fully experience the impact we had on the world.

Unlike the current reward and punishment system that promises paradise for the good or damnation for the wicked, the Universe allows you to feel your impact and contributions as a human instead. This method is highly effective for our spirit's enlightenment.

This is why the Universe will never judge or damn you. The worst we could experience exists on planet Earth not in the spiritual realm.

God and the Devil are symbols for the light and dark energies of the Universe. They are words we use to represent an idea. God represents good. Satan or the Devil represents evil. This makes it easy for humans to grasp the symbolism.

At the time of transition from physical form back to spiritual, Source or the Universe understands that we lived a human life, and even though we're beautiful beings, we are flawed. We're allowed to make mistakes to learn from them. Mistakes are one of the primary ways of learning and gaining knowledge.

We're allowed to choose the type of person we want to be in this world on the spectrum of beneficial to detrimental. We're expected to be tempted by sex, money, and power…or drawn to companionship, objects, and status, which are all part of the human experience.

Sex, money, and power are not bad words. They are

not evil. They are a part of our world, societies and our makeup. It's what we do with them that determines where it stands on the spectrum of good or bad.

We can wield our power to access abundance and prosperity for an entire society. Or we can use our power to corrupt. We choose.

So why would the Universe punish us for being human and having human instincts if this is all part of the human experience?

Spirit doesn't judge. Humans do. And in our spirit form, after we complete our life on Earth, we will experience, feel, and understand the total impact of every decision we made while on Earth. And we are free to judge our actions as we see fit for our enlightenment. Afterall, this is the point in having a human experience.

Spirit doesn't judge us for writing erotica, reading tarot, having sex, or any other so-called "sin." The intention of life is to understand, evolve and aid and benefit others in their growth and doing so is not meant to be easy.

Afterall, no one's perfect. We all must eat, sleep and shit.

END OF CHANNELED MESSAGE

Chapter 7

The Book Block

THE CHAPTER TITLE stares back at me from the laptop. I'm proud of myself for making it this far in the story, no matter how difficult getting back into writing has become.

It was because of Spirit that this book's idea came to be. I knew the year 2025 would be a big year for me and humanity, but even I didn't want to believe it. I sensed the spiritual battle of ultimate "good" versus "evil" long before the 2024 presidential election. I knew we'd be faced with the ultimate test of deciding the fate of the American empire. I'm not surprised, only disappointed, in America's decision.

Evil had *apparently* won.

I've been anxious and depressed ever since.

I know a lot of things, especially that nothing will keep me down. I'm in an enlightened part of my human journey where I realize life is a series of ebbs and flows. What goes up must come down, but once at rock bottom there's only one way to go from there. We never stay in the puddle, because the mud eventually dries up.

Just as Earth's duality promises the opposite ends of the spectrum, karma promises a return on our investment. We get what we give. What we put out eventually returns to us. Dualism is necessary for the balance and stability of Earth's existence.

Even though I'm aware of this, I still fear the unknown.

I used to be able to write and create characters, worlds, and get into the state of creative flow. But now, writing has become a struggle. However, putting words on the page is hard to do because my fear limits me and causes doubt. Just another way of draining my power.

The fear of failure, being judged, being attacked, being wrong is meant to chip away at my power and prevent me from writing these very words. That anxiety comes from trying to please society and not challenging what others believe is true, understandable, and acceptable.

After weeks of trying to prevent a creative breakdown while in the midst of one, knowing nothing about where I was headed but insisting on severing the thread that connected me to my past, I declared I was done.

Not done with writing. Never. Even if I wrote for my eyes only or for free, I'd still do it, because I don't write strictly for the money. I write to express myself, because I have a lot to say.

Even as a kid, fantasizing about my future as an author, it was the possibility that others would one day read my words that excited and fueled me. How else could I get anyone to listen?

Of course, I'd like to make a living from my creations. However, money isn't what drives me.

No, I realized I was done with the current state of the publishing industry.

I had run across online statistics that showed the lack of diversity in the traditional publishing space, from the editors that handpick the manuscripts, to the authors that have their books chosen for publication, to the books that are published, and all the way to the reviewers who promoted them. Across the board, the lack of diversity meant the demographics of who got the opportunities or benefited the most in the industry were straight, white, cis, nondisabled women. The demographic with the least opportunities in traditional publishing, reviews and promotion were Black women.

None of this is new.

Black women are statically the least cared for, trusted, helped or believed in America and I'd argue even globally. Apparently, according to humanity's agreed upon rules of life, Black folks are the most feared, hated, and misunderstood race and women are the most disrespected, silenced and mistreated gender.

That information made me take a step back and look at the state of the publishing industry. Finally, I understood the reason I watched a lot of my peers get publishing opportunities and success, while I clapped on the sidelines awaiting my chance. I refused to write the trends, tropes or do what everyone else was doing, also, I am a Black female.

Conforming, as I did to write the previous book that caused my burnout and hatred of the industry, felt like selling out or selling my soul. And metaphorically, the struggle through the hardship of burnout, was me trying to find my soul again.

If it didn't come from my heart, it felt forced and became a detriment.

When suddenly, out of the blue, an old friend reached out online after years of silence. They gave a short greeting and an even shorter question: Are you familiar with writing biographies?

I gave an honest answer: No, I write fiction because I enjoy creating characters and worlds.

Then they explained how they were in the middle of writing their own biography. It's not unusual to hear this a lot as a writer. Family, friends and even strangers often express how they believe their life would make a good story. The conversation usually ends with, "If you need any story ideas, let me know. My life would make a good book."

But Spirit works in this way, nudging me in the right direction by placing an idea on my path through signs, symbols and synchronicity. I just didn't know it at the time.

Days later, my frustrations with my lack of creative progress and my growing hatred for the state of the publishing industry and the state of my country birthed an unusual idea.

Most fiction looked the same in the industry. If the statistic are saying the same types of publishers put out the same types of books in the same types of genres written by the same types of authors which are reviewed by the same types of reviewers who promote to the same types of readers, then continuing to try to pursue a spot where statistically it was impossible for me to debut or thrive sounded insane.

It's time to consider publishing nonfiction.

Sure, I've gotten a few articles published where I shared knowledge on the writing business and publishing industry, but I've never written a nonfiction book. However, the flood of similar types of stories being published, recommended and read in fiction, made the decision to transition a bit easier.

What would I write about?

My growing fear of artificial intelligence dominating the creative space and the rapid rise of its use in creative writing reminded me that authenticity will be the way to thrive artistically. Ai will become so mainstream that people will eventually begin seeking out real, honest, authentic artists and art. And what could I write in a way that Ai couldn't?

My story is unique to me and only I can share it in my voice, and that's what makes it special. Telling my story my way is something no one, not even Ai, can do.

I think I'm ready to make a shift and tell my story.

This will be one of your most difficult projects. It requires you to be vulnerable, open and honest in ways you've never been. Over the entirety of this year, you'll come to terms with that.

As of writing this, I have come to terms with that. I've gotten so much insight and information over the months that I no longer doubt that I chose this as my life's purpose.

I know this because I'm fully embodying my power. I've done the internal work, digging deep within me though meditation and self-reflection to discover who I really am. I've scrutinized and studied each of my many masks, understanding myself much more each day.

Over the last year, I've come to realize a highly empowering truth. Black females may be the most mistreated, disrespected, misunderstood and hated due to others' fear.

Fear of our power!

Disregarding Black females, our voice, and our contributions are ways of making us small, keeping us down, dimming our light, and preventing us from discovering our true power and potential.

We are far from our stereotypes and labels. If Black females are so lazy, why did colonizers kidnap and enslave them to work the fields and care for their families? If we are so dangerous, why did they force Black women to be caregivers and cooks? If we're such disgusting savages, why were Black women forced to nurse their infants from their own breasts?

The truth is, Black people are so powerful we set trends, inspire change, and are imitated in every industry with our beauty, fashion, music, dance, culture and more. Our clothing choices, hair styles, physique, appearances and even anatomy are often copied by others. Our mannerisms, swag, accents, personalities, and talents are often appropriated and exploited for profit. Our ideas, insights, and creations are undervalued in our presence but highly sought after without credit.

Being exactly who I am out loud and proud, by unapologetically shedding the masks, is the best gift I can unwrap.

Spirit uses our ego and our human desires to steer us down paths to fulfillment. I used to believe wanting respect and recognition for my writing was a bad thing because it was egotistical or selfish. That is false. It is what motivates my human body and mind to pursue my spiritual purpose. And it aligns with my mission to write books that bring knowledge of the spiritual and physical to the world.

In this regard, my urge for respect and recognition is the motivation I need as a human to push me closer to fulfilling my spiritual goal. Therefore, the ego and spiritual work together.

I do not believe we must get rid of our ego. We must learn why it exists and work with it.

Our human needs, wants, and desires are not inherently bad. They are necessary for our growth. Just as negative experiences in life shows us what we can get through and teaches us strength and resilience.

I understand why I chose to enter Earth school as a Black female in America at the time I did. The adversity I've experienced throughout my life and the usual disregard for the Black female did not make me a victim but a force to be reckoned with.

When in sixth grade, I first discovered a well-known horror anthology book. And at that moment, I knew I wanted to be an author. The cover of the anthology was unique and special, making me realize it probably shouldn't be in a children's library. The creepy illustrations frightened yet empowered me. Knowing a book like that exists meant there was a possibility I could do it too.

Though I didn't realize it at the time, that had been my dream all along, ever since Mama's creepy tales hit my ears as a child. And what I've come to realize is I did not only want to see my name on a book cover or become a well-known author but also create something that was my own. I needed to stand out and write what may be considered controversial and possibly talked about for years to come for inspiring others to see their potential.

This urge came about because I didn't see just a book. I saw that book's impact long before it manifested. I could see how it would inspire many children to become authors, writers and express themselves the way they wanted. I saw the ripple effect of how new authors would be born to love, promote and create horror tales that would captivate and inspire even more people to come.

I recognized the book's power. I saw what it would become. How teachers, parents, adults and authority would claim it was a book they should shield the children from. They would call it "the Devil's work." They would declare it "too scary for children," "too twisted" and believe it would twist young minds and create troublemakers.

Those things make the book much more special and I knew that when I picked it up. I sensed the book's power and all its potential, and that's what drew me in.

Why do we admire certain celebrities? Why do we follow their lives and career, and feel so drawn to their stories?

Because they are mirrors reflecting our own traits, characteristics or behavior.

I admire one of the biggest selling Black women in the music industry. She's captivating, beautiful, and magnetic. No matter what she does we can't take our eyes from her. She comes off as an amazing mother. She projects femininity and an amazing power, and that power has inspired so many people across the globe. She makes beautiful art, beautiful music. She has a voice that can stop someone in their tracks.

She is so powerful, she attracts people who try to take that power from her with hate of her, her music, and everything she stands for. Many tried to strip her of her authenticity by claiming her pregnancy was faked, she can't really sing, and insisting she stays in her lane.

Many try to take her power because it's so immense.

And not only that, but I admire her because she's also responsible and generous with her wealth. She has gratitude for her family and the things that got her in her elevated position. She's on top. She's the queen.

The traits we admire in a celebrity are the traits we possess ourselves. We wish to embody those characteristics. We can see ourselves acquiring those attributes. That power. We see ourselves in our favorite celebrities. And if we as physical beings do not, our spirit self does. They recognize and are attracted to those qualities.

This is also the reason why I was so attracted to that popular horror anthology book. I admire those traits that made the anthology so memorable and aimed to create a book just like it because of what it represents. My own story might be controversial, impact lives, inspire many people, and be talked about for decades to come.

And I finally understand that, seeing how the Universe works to lead me where I need to be to grant my wishes.

I also see the potential in others as well, and that's how I interact with people. I sense the power and potential that resides within them. My spirit meets their spirit, and I acknowledge it even if they haven't recognized their own power, potential and spirit yet—the higher self within all of us.

And so, I give most people the benefit of the doubt. I inspire others to go after their goals. When I identify what their human is lacking and in need of, even if it's attention and validation, I provide that. When they get what they are seeking, it can lead to them recognizing their power.

I do my best to uplift them. Anything to let them know they could do everything they want in life. I provide what they need because I'm not judging them or their actions as a human, I connect with their potential, their soul, their higher self, their spirit that patiently awaits their acknowledgement.

Our soul wants to co-create with us. It wants to guide us, along with our team of spiritual helpers, towards the life we wish to live.

Spirit is never dormant.

Occasionally, Spirit tries to communicate. We'll feel their messages in our heart or gut. Unexpectedly, we will recognize their language, signs, symbols and synchronicities. Even if we're unable to distinguish the signs, or we're unaware of our ability to understand the language and interpret the message, Spirit will continue to connect knowing one day something profound will spark the power within us. Spirit patiently waits for that day.

Our spirit guides, higher self, and angels interfere at pivotal times in our lives when they must disrupt, protect or guide. These are nudges, a push or prod, an invitation awaiting our welcome. We only have to recognize it's there, that it exists.

If we look back at our past at strange yet life-changing moments to realize something just lined up perfectly to provide us what we needed at the exact time we needed it. That is our spirit, our guides, the Universe. And they're waiting for us to say, "You know what? I see you."

When we get called from Spirit to act or pursue, to speak up, to make change or get a sudden stirring in our heart and know deep inside it's the right thing to do, follow it. If we can envision how certain decisions would pull us out of a rut or lead us down a path that we needed to go, yet we meet it with debilitating fear. The heaviness of fear becomes an obstacle, holding us down and preventing us from moving forward. When fear stops you in your tracks from going down the best path, that's a sign that this is the path we desperately need to pursue.

This book is one of those pivotal moments where it could change our life for the rest of our life. This is when we listen to that voice within, our higher self, our soul, our spirit, the Universe, and answer by acknowledging its existence within us. That power.

These words come to me from one of my bathtime channeling sessions. While I relax in a lavender scented bubble bath, I allow the words to flow because I know this is how Spirit wants to co-create with me to help me write this book.

This is our method.

This is my spiritual team's way of showing me I'm on the right path and this is what I'm meant to do. While also showing how important it is that I complete this book and my purpose. They helped me follow through, share my knowledge, and not be afraid.

I'm deathly afraid.

I'm fearful of people's judgment. So many will see me for who I really am, with my masks off, and they possibly won't like what they see. I'm afraid of being labeled as crazy. I'm terrified that I may be harmed in some way, I will be silenced. However, that fear is proof that this is what I need to do. It reflects how important my mission is and demonstrates that this is exactly what I need to do.

Spirit has my back. They assure me over and over that this

project would be a success. In every pick-a-card tarot reading I watch, no matter which message I listen to, they keep repeating with signs, symbols and synchronicities that this is what I need to do.

I'm on the right path.

I will reach the right people. My voice will be heard around the world, and it will change lives and inspire so many. These words will awaken many people and allow them to connect with their higher consciousness so we can make massive changes and get this world back on track, stable, balanced and where it needs to be to create the unity and harmony we wish to see in the world.

I get so deep into channeling that I start talking and lose track of what I was saying. When I snap out of it, I realize I don't remember what I just said. Thank the heavens I voice record during bathtime sessions. There's always so much information coming through.

I allow my higher self to speak through me to bring this book from the spiritual into the physical or material manifestation. Spirit keeps stressing the importance of this work and the importance of sharing the details of how it was created.

I think that importance is what scares me because I don't want to mess it up. But they keep reassuring me through everything I see and hear, listen to and read, that everything is going to work out. They promise there is no need to fear. That I would look back at this moment one day and laugh at how scared I was.

I'm stripping away the layers, taking off all the masks, and standing spiritually naked in front of everyone. That's a scary thing for a human to do. It's scary because for so long society always told us that being naked in front of a crowd was wrong, was a bad thing that would be judged and persecuted and looked down upon, frowned at and judged. And that prevents us from doing it. We conform, give away our power. Fear diminishes our power and soon we diminish our own power for the sake of fitting in.

That's where we're our weakest and powerless, without a voice. Just sheep. Following each other, the trends, mainstream, and the leader. Becoming like everyone else, forgetting how powerful we are and that we could literally change and create worlds.

That's why one of the most common nightmares is being naked in front of a crowd, because it triggers our deepest fear of being judged. Planted in our minds by those who want to control us and keep us from knowing our power.

And the more we understand that the more we realize the importance of authenticity. Being authentic allows us to be comfortable in our skin and not care what others have to say.

I don't need validation. I don't need to prove myself. I don't need the world to tell me I'm right. I'm not afraid to be told I'm wrong. Because the proof is in the pudding.

Their heart, soul and power will activate upon reading these words because they'll realize the truth. Their heart will beat faster, harder, and ache as proof. They will realize the sensation is the power within them, their higher self, reaching out to announce its presence, asking for an invitation to co-create.

I'm ready, but how do I start?

Just be you. Your knowledge will help many.

Chapter 8

Trusting is Tough

TRUSTING MY INTUITION and inner calling is difficult even as I write this very sentence. I struggle, going back and forth wondering if I'm making all of this up. What if it's all in my head? Because I'm present in two worlds, my physical and my spiritual side, the earthly, logical side of me is also skeptical and doubtful, questioning and analyzing everything including my own intuition.

The proof is in the pudding.

You are meant to be a walking, talking, living, breathing testimony.

I was born into Earth school, starting out in poor condition, but turned that difficult start into success. Being born Black and female with an abusive childhood, teenage pregnancy, high school dropout, unstable low-income, debt, and an abusive romantic relationship—the data pointed me toward remaining in poverty, ending up in jail or an early death.

The likelihood of a person coming from that dire state to end up embracing her Black femininity, healing her inner child, breaking the teen pregnancy cycle within her own immediate family, becoming highly educated with a stable income, and a truly loving marriage is low.

But I did it.

For me to truly trust Spirit meant I need measurable proof. My earthly side always searches for more knowledge on any topic to form my own opinions. Even when Spirit provides undeniable proof of their assistance, my human side still doubts.

In 2006, at twenty-four years old, I had an unforgettable encounter with an angel that forever cemented my beliefs in them. I received a gift that changed everything, even though I hadn't realized it at the time, an innocent book of angels by a world-renowned psychic.

I needed a distraction from the daily struggle of transitioning from a long-term relationship to becoming a single mother, taking on one hundred percent of the responsibilities.

Determined to give my kids a good life, me and my two baby girls moved into a studio apartment. The small space connected to a cramped kitchen where my babies sat on the floor in front of the oven to eat their meals since the lack of space didn't allow for a dining table.

The living room was also our bedroom, where I inflated a queen size air mattress for the three-year-old and five-year-old to sleep on while I lay on the longer of the two couches.

I read the entire book that night. During the final pages, readers could recite a prayer to invite angels in. So, I did it. I recited the words and set an intention for an angel visitation.

Since it was getting late and the kids were asleep, I called it a night. The kitchen light stayed on to act as a nightlight in case any of us awakened in the middle of the night for the bathroom. I snuggled into the couch, stuffing my face near the rear cushions as my back faced the open room. A thin blanket acted as my warmth and protection as I closed my eyes.

Suddenly, the energy surrounding me changed and I no longer felt like it was only me and my girls in the room.

Another's presence filled the space, and the sensation of someone watching me hit me. The first thing that entered my mind was someone else was in my apartment. While facing the back of the couch, lying on my side, I slowly turned my head to peek over my shoulder.

Fear raced through me as the light from the kitchen cast a shadow that stretched along one entire wall of a giant, feathered wing. I questioned if it was an image of a wing, and maybe the light caught one of the kid's toys or something. Then the wing moved as if attached to a body. The tip of the wing furled outward slightly.

I freaked out.

I buried my face in the back of the couch as my heartbeat sped up and panic paralyzed me. The only thing going through my head at the time was, "What did I invite into my house?!"

Had I summoned something I wasn't prepared for? What was I doing? Sweating, heart racing, I was amid a full-on panic attack. "What do I do? What do I do? What do I do?!"

Out of nowhere, a comforting hand rested on my shoulder. Yet the sensations were so gentle it seemed as if the hand hovered, while the soothing energy flowed through me. As I absorbed the energy, a warm, calm and loving feeling rushed over me. Then I heard her reassuring voice, but not through my ears. "It's ok. It's alright. You're ok." The instant relief at the sound of the voice, touch and words was a mix of an unexplainable encouraging feeling I'll never forget.

She surrounded me in a pure love that felt like no human has ever experienced. The warmth was like being bathed in a tub of warm, liquid love. Encompassing, uplifting, relaxing. I just wanted to surrender, let go and exist. And so, I did.

Then bright white light flooded the space around me.

I sensed her nurturing femininity and her angelic power as she continually assured me that I was in good hands. She didn't even have to say the words. Her embrace communicated her intentions.

It felt so good, tears of gratitude rolled down my face. It was the best sensation ever. I've never experienced a feeling like that in my entire life. I didn't even know that feeling existed until that very moment.

Truly amazing.

The next moment was like a time shift and then everything changed. I abruptly sat up on the couch and looked around to see my typical studio apartment. The light still shone from the kitchen, the girls were still asleep, and there was no longer a huge wing shadow on the wall.

What was that? What did I just experience?

For years to come, I thought I was crazy. I made excuses, falling back into society's norms of dismissing the experiences we can't explain. I told no one, kept it to myself as if it was an odd dream.

What I didn't realize was I was in denial. I didn't really want to believe an angel had visited me because I was afraid of what others would think. Afraid they would label me crazy or insane. I was fearful of embarrassing myself.

Fear has a way of keeping us boxed in our comfort zones.

But that visitation stayed with me for years. I eventually told two people, my cousin and my husband.

Going from being indoctrinated into religion, being told I'm a Baptist and not really understanding what that meant, I started looking into religion and became increasingly uncomfortable with its use to control. There was a period where I became agnostic. I believed there was a greater purpose to life, but I stopped subscribing to man's definition of God.

Then I learned about the Soviet Cosmonauts and the Salut Seven Space Station, about a group of cosmonauts who had an encounter in space with what they called Angels. And they experienced some of the things I experienced with my angelic visitation, especially that overwhelming feeling of calm, love and warmth.

That triggered a realization in me.

Have others experienced the same thing I had? Was my angel visitation real? That was the day I knew, this was something bigger than just my imagination.

Even then, so many synchronicities happened to lead me to research near death experiences. When I questioned the visit, commercials about visiting angels would come on TV, or my favorite show would mention near death experiences, feathers would appear when I needed confirmation and more.

With near death experiences, or NDEs, the people

who died and were revived reported the same angelic visits, occurrences and sensations when they passed over into the spiritual realm.

The one thing that fascinated me about those stories was what they described feeling because I felt that too. Whenever they try to describe the love it's difficult, because words can never do it justice.

That's when I knew my angel experience was real. And I feel so lucky to have had that experience. It doesn't happen every day or for many people. So many may never get that experience, and because of that I view it as sacred. I don't want to ask for another angel visitation. I didn't want to play around with such a profound experience. It was a cherished moment I don't want to ruin by turning it into a game or a joke.

It stayed with me all these years and it's something I don't think anyone who has experienced something similar would ever forget.

It took so many years, signs, symbols and synchronicity, but it was required to teach me to trust my intuition and my inner knowing. Doing so was just the beginning of stepping into my power and creating the life I wanted.

CHANNELED MESSAGE ABOUT MANIFESTATION JUST FOR YOU

The real secret to manifestation and the law of attraction is action, not only making your thoughts positive, stating what you want clearly, letting it go and sending it out to the Universe. Those are symbolic and metaphors for how to take action to make it happen.

First you have to know what you want and be clear, like wishing upon a star. That is setting your wish into motion. Making that wish by vocalizing it. Once you vocalize it, you can even refine it to make sure you know exactly what your wish is and what you want to acquire.

The next step is to believe. As simple as it sounds it is hard to do. Because this is where people start doubting and letting logic get in the way. And it clouds their belief, making it unclear on what they really want and if they could obtain it. So, you must work hard and even extra hard to maintain belief. It's a deep knowing. It's seeing who you really are, what you have, the power you possess, and you have what it takes to do anything you want in this life. That's what belief is. Believing in yourself, the dream, believe that this is your destiny that you're writing it in the stars, co-creating with the Creator, with the Universe.

Belief is a powerful tool. Just as thoughts are when creating, because what you focus on is what you create in your world and it's not by magic. It's because you focus on it so much that the energy of it, the emotions it brings, formulate the circumstances you live in and go through. Therefore, it's like a self-fulfilling prophecy when you focus on the bad, the negative. That's why your belief and thoughts should remain positive. And even that is hard to do. That's why this step takes skills, but once you become an expert, the next step is to take action.

These are several tiers. To take action will require you

to know the steps needed to get to your goal. You think of your dream, you wish, what did you want? And you think of every detail about it. For example, it's to live in a beautiful house by the ocean, content, happy, fulfilled. Now think backwards from that future scene all the way back to where you are now in step one. And then formulate, in your mind or on paper, how to get up the steps of that stairway to your wish.

Start with where you are today and what you can do tomorrow to get closer to that wish. Maybe the one step is research, finding out where you want to live. What coastal places feel like home to you? The next step is to visit that place and see if it feels right in your heart. Remember, your heart knows. It will pitter patter. Your gut will heat up. Your heart jolts when faced with truth. That's why they say follow your heart because your heart will lead you.

So, follow each step, place it down like a plank on a staircase that elevates you closer to that wish, right next to the star you wished upon. That is manifestation. That is how you make your dreams come true.

Always take action. Nothing will ever just fall into your lap. Not a thing that will lead to your dreams, to your true calling, to your true wish fulfillment. It won't just tumble into your lap. You will have to take action. You will have to make a plan. You will have to put in mental energy, research and readiness, preparing yourself inside and out.

Mental and emotional action is just as important as the physical action you take.

The deeper you go inside yourself, the more you will want to fix, change, and improve yourself and your life. Self-reflect while in the bath, resting, relaxing, and allow peace, solitude and clarity to come in. Go inside yourself while taking a leisurely walk down a secluded path, skating, biking or on a long car ride. These are moments where you can zone out, tune in, and figure out who you really are. Delve deep into why you believe the things you believe. Why do you like or dislike the things you like or dislike? Why do you feel a particular way toward certain people? Why are you attracted to a specific type of person? Why do you yearn for success in a specific field or career? Why do you have certain talents?

Even work on your shadow self or the subconscious. The painful things kept hidden away. It could be traumas, fears, and insecurities. Dig deep into those things and understand why they exist. Go back further and deeper. Ask important questions. Why, how? Why didn't I? Why did? Who? When? These are questions to seek. All these questions, once answered, will get you closer to the root. Because everything grows from the root. And if there's root rot, it may not bear fruit. So go to that root to figure out what caused the rot. Dig deep because facing your shadow self and doing that shadow work is going to transform your life in more ways than one.

That is part of introspection and getting to the root of the cause because now you know it's capable of rot, and future seeds would avoid the same pitfalls when planted. And moving forward, you are on your way to healing, becoming whole again, finding your power, harnessing it, and wielding it to create the physical world you want.

The more honest you are with yourself, going deep into meditations, yoga practices or quietly sipping tea on the balcony, the more epiphanies you'll have. Out of nowhere you will get ideas, insight, truth. And you will realize the real world you've been living in. And the more you strip away what shaped you and the veneer you showcase to the world, the more you understand the world around you also has a veneer.

It is a veneer placed on the people and the world. And now you have clarity. Now you can see the truth for what it is. Not only truth within yourself but also in the outside world. And once you see that truth, it will lead to major transformation because this is a part of your life where you're going to start backing away from what society deems "normal." You're going to stop following the trends and stop caring about what others think. Because you'll start realizing many people think the way society, their parents, their family, the government, the media and their peers think.

You will start to see everyone around you has a veneer too. So, the things that they say aren't even coming from an authentic place. You won't let the words and the negativity of the outside world seep in. You will back away. You will reflect more. You will understand what you need to do to grow and change. You may back away from relationships. You may change career fields.

Things will switch quickly because you're following your heart and what's true.

And this is further shaping you so you can further shape your life.

Now that the veneer has been shattered from the world around you. You can see how you can shape that world to create the world you want to live in. You can see where the trails lead, and where the roots grow and how they connect with one another and how they form and create. You can even go back in other people's lives, starting with the decisions they made, and dig deep until you see their truth. And then you would become so aware that you can see it in an instant. You'll no longer have to think, analyze and peel away the layers. You see it. You see people and who they truly are, but that could be scary because a lot of people are not good people.

A lot of people have hatred toward you, are jealous, wish for your downfall, want to see you in pain. And it hurts because some are people you love. Your friends, family, or parents. Some are your priest, teacher, or your doctor and it will hurt. But by this time, you know your worth, you know who you are, and you know your power. You're harnessing your power and wielding that power, not letting any of that affect you negatively anymore. You're grateful for seeing everyone for who they truly are. And you're thankful to have that gift even though it comes with that caveat. You accept it. It's part of what makes you empathetic and compassionate. And you need these things to create your world. Because your world is created from the energy of compassion, empathy and love. And once you tap into that, nothing can stop you.

END OF CHANNELED MESSAGE

Chapter 9

The Tree of Life

A TREE IS MADE up of several parts, but mainly the roots, the trunk and the branches. Imagine life as a tree, the branches are your possible paths, and the goal is to make it to the top.

As I mentioned previously, before our birth on Earth, we were spirit on the other side, and we planned our human experiences alongside our spiritual mentors. We determined what lessons we needed to learn and the situations we would encounter to gain knowledge. The goal is to pass our lessons like quizzes.

We each have a purpose, fated events, experiences and opportunities, yet our free will allows us to choose how to accomplish them. Therefore, fate and freewill exist at the same time. So, if our physical body's life begins at the trunk of the tree, and our goal is to get to the top, our freewill allows us the many branches to choose from to get there. Every branch is its own path and the right path, yet at times we may get "lost."

In moments of misdirection, our spirit team steps in to guide us. They will send signs, symbols and synchronicities or meaningful coincidences to open the gates of communication. This is an invitation. We decide to respond to it or not. If we miss the signs, sometimes our guides will nudge us, gently tapping our shoulder like a friendly tutor or bestie throwing us a hint or a peek at the answers to a quiz.

For example, while channeling during a bathtime session, I began wondering how divine interventions happen to direct us on the correct path. I sang along with the music playing and tuned into the visual playing out in my mind's eye.

The song was an emotional power ballad from one of the best female vocalists and songwriters of all time. As a child in the 80s, I had connected to the magnetism of this musical artist and her talent, becoming a fan ever since. Her beauty captivated me as I thought she looked a lot like my oldest sister, especially their skin tone and hair texture.

Ever since her song debuted while I was in middle school, it was my favorite.

Then I began thinking about middle school. Back then, a few friends tried to convince the quiet-reserve-wallflower to join Chorus, insisting that I would only have to sing a snippet of any song so the instructor could place me by my vocal register.

I didn't have the courage to sing in front of anyone at school, yet throughout my life, music was always a huge part. I joined Band to play the clarinet. I became the only female vocalist of a hip-hop group with my older half-brother and my cousin. Together we wrote and recorded several tracks. Later, I wrote and recorded my own songs.

Music was another way for me to express myself and fulfill my purpose. Yet I decided to climb the branches that aligned me toward the path of writing. And those branches supported me, because either path led toward the same goal, inspiring others through creative expression.

And those paths are always available.

We decide which branches to climb. The Universe only nudges us in the most beneficial direction.

If we acknowledge the signs and learn to develop communication with our spirit guides, we become more fluent in the language of intuition and use the guidance to lead us along our path toward the top of the tree to our goal.

To become fluent in the language of spirit, we must go within. Our higher self, the spirit self, is our power. Coming into union with our higher self allows us the power to co-create whatever we desire in physical life and advance our higher self toward enlightenment.

In moments of solitude or self-isolation, go within. Take time to tune into emotions and mental health. Rest, relax and take time to heal the physical body. Meditate and do breathwork to become calm and centered. Then ask questions and answer them honestly.

Do the shadow work of healing past wounds, false beliefs, and identify what is preventing progress. Set boundaries, discover our worth, let go of people, places and things that don't align with your values or keep us stuck. Then emerge one day from that isolation a changed person.

If for some reason we didn't learn the lesson we were meant to, like all cycles in life, it will return. We will find ourselves in the same or similar situation until we learn what that experience is trying to teach us. Once we implement the lesson, circumstances change.

Like staying in toxic relationships. Every red flag warns of the danger, yet it's ignored. Those signs will remain until recognized. Even if we manage to do the right thing and end the relationship, we will be tested. The Universe will put a similar person on our path, and the cycle continues until we learn and make a change.

It happens this way for our growth.

Think of it like the school tutor showing the same math problem using different numbers. Did we remember how to get to the answer? If not, we must relearn the lesson by going through the steps again. Once we get it right, we are rewarded with progress, knowledge, and power that will get us closer to our desires.

Once you know better, do better.

Having to repeat cycles are never punishments for making the wrong choice, that's Karma's role.

The tree's roots represent our subconscious, where we dig deep and go within. The roots reside within us, in our past, our childhood, our ancestry and generational cycles. The roots of any plant must be healthy and sturdy to support the flowering plant and provide abundant fruits.

Identify the issues that are creating false truths. Recognize the wounds we still carry like heavy baggage. Heal those parts any way we can through the help of professionals like doctors and therapists, and/or healers, spiritual teachers and educators. Read books, study philosophies, ask questions and find the answers.

Once the roots are healthy, the tree can provide stable branches to climb and get to the ample fruit at the top.

CHANNELED MESSAGE ABOUT AUTHENTICITY JUST FOR YOU

Before you can get to the place we want to go, or accomplish our major life goals, you must first know who you are. To do that, you must go within to understand any problem and tackle it. Then you can move toward taking action to achieve your goals and fulfill your wishes.

Go within to shape your reality.

A lot of us aren't living in our authenticity. This is why we surf the internet and are addicted to social media because it allows us to be whoever we want to be, and most of the time we aren't being ourselves. That's because most of us don't know who we truly are. We learned to put on layers, masks and bodysuits to mirror what society, our parents, our peers, and others wants us to be. The way we fit in and feel love, acceptance and seen is by putting on a veneer to show the world, but it keeps us trapped in more ways than one, especially when it comes to fulfilling our dreams.

We get lost in trying to please others, in trying to be the best version of ourselves by seeking things that we think are success. Success is a word we place on our goals, aspirations and dreams that others decide for us because of our need to conform in a society, a group, or a community. We change who we are, and we can't get ahead and meet our life's goals or even fulfill our life's purpose until we go deep inside, do some introspection and learn who we truly are. That requires stripping away layers. The first layer is your primary issue in your life.

What are you doing or not doing right now that makes you feel stuck? Go deep into the reason. Ask yourself, how did I get here? Be honest, be real, because only you will hear the answer. No one else can judge, embarrass or shame you. Be true to yourself about your answers. Don't try to sugarcoat it or change it into a more acceptable answer. Say it the way you feel it, and then go deeper, because you will have more questions arise after you answer them. Answer those questions and the next until you get to the root cause of this issue.

For example, if you're having a falling-out with your friend and you asked yourself why you can't seem to get along. Delve into your part of the story, your perspective. What happened? What could have triggered that separation? Be honest with yourself.

Did you distance yourself first? Did you leave that person out? Did you lie about that person? Just be real and then go deeper. Why did you lie? And be truthful and be honest. Because you were jealous. You were upset that they get things so easily. You wanted them to know how it feels to lose. And then go deeper. Why did you feel this way? What does this stem from? Maybe the cause is your lack of faith in friendships.

That's an honest answer that you could delve deeper into to get to the root of the problem.

Why do you feel that way? Is it because you were raised in a household, a country or a society where those certain beliefs are the norm? And if you want to go further into how this all originated with you, go even deeper until you feel like you can't dig anymore and you hit the root cause. And once you hit the root cause, you will feel it in your chest because your heart doesn't lie. You will know the true reason your friendship disintegrated. And now you can work on what you need to do to resolve the issue.

Would apologizing help? Would being honest with your friend help the situation? If you think that will fix the issue, you discovered the key.

The key will lead you forward through a doorway where you are able to manifest the life you want. Manifest your dreams, your goals, where you want to be, how much money you want to make, what partner you want beside you. That one session of honest introspection gives you the key. With the key, decide to do better. Take accountability and responsibility and improve yourself, because once you know the truth there's no turning back.

You will never encounter a similar situation without facing the truth head on. Once you recognize the pattern, it's up to you to break it.

END OF CHANNELED MESSAGE

Chapter 10

Toxic Love

BATTLED WITH MYSELF on how to approach this next chapter. As I wanted to leave names, locations, and details out. As I questioned if I should include it at all. But while I was thinking, I got some insight.

This part of your story is the most important

Why?

This will be the part that resonates with most people.

How much details should I share?

You don't have to share any details at all. Just share your story.

As I sit writing these very words, a vision popped into my head of me leaving such a legacy in the world that a movie is made about my life. Then I stopped daydreaming and laughed, telling myself, "No. That wasn't a premonition. I don't predict future events."

And then, in my mind, I heard, "Why not? If you dream it, you will it."

For a moment, I considered...yes. Why not? If that's to be my future, so be it. But then I laughed, imagining this very moment. "The movie will depict me sitting here at an oversized, dirty desk, with drops of fast-food sauce, a stick of deodorant and prescription pill bottles scattered across it. They'll overdramatize my alopecia and anxiety. They would have me at my desk with my rapidly bouncing leg, using my fingernail to pick my teeth, looking baldheaded while talking to myself and my angels." I laughed and felt the angels laugh too.

But then it was back to writing these very words. Distracted from the fact that I had to make decisions on how to handle this next part.

While wondering how to proceed with this chapter, I allowed my ego or my human-self to chime in. My ego urges to add in details, list names and particular events, but then I'm reminded:

Will doing so help you accomplish your purpose?

I could probably tell my story more creatively, without putting anyone on blast.

If you get lost, focus on your purpose.

My purpose. Not the hell others put me through, the toxicity, the dysfunction, unless it will help others.

I surrendered, because I know I'm enlightened enough to integrate with my power, my higher self, and make the decisions my higher self would. Or, in short. I know better, therefore I do better.

Toxicity. An energy I'm all too familiar with. Sometimes it appears as gossip making its rounds before finally coming around to me. Other times it shows up as animosity or resentment, holding my actions and mistakes against me for years. At other times it comes out as backhanded compliments, or a blatant disregard of my accomplishments. A lot of times it appears as awkward silence when I enter a packed room.

Being in tune with the vibes, I'd always pick up on it. The sly grins, the snarky eye rolls, the clear disinterest. My inner self reminds me that I choose how to respond, and I learned to not acknowledge it and keep it moving. I recently heard a saying: if someone tries to hand you a gift but you refuse it, is it theirs or yours? Theirs. So, when someone tries to give you embarrassment, shame or disrespect, don't accept it. Don't acknowledge it or react to it. Let them keep it.

Which after many decades, I learned to do.

How many people grow up stitched to their mom and seven siblings' side to end up disconnected and isolated from them later in life? Not just me, I'm sure.

I've recently come to learn that reciprocity is very important in every relationship, be it romantic, platonic, parental, familial, or business. Connections become one sided and draining when the weight of the relationship is left for one person to carry.

So as of writing this, I have isolated myself from my extended family. I never had any true friends to release, I only had to stay off social media to establish that boundary.

Over the last few months, before writing this, I had come into some clarity. My deep spiritual work and self-reflection showed me where I needed to improve and what and who I needed to remove from my life for my growth.

I quickly learned how to reinforce boundaries. I let go of so many one-sided relationships, most of them at the same time. Gone were the connections that left me feeling neglected, used, manipulated or abused. All the people that constantly ask but refuse to give or those who have a lot to say but never an ear to listen. If the relationship felt like an obligation, I let it go.

I've spent decades of my life being helpful, generous, and respectful. I've been a shoulder to cry on, an insightful advisor, and an open wallet to people who failed to respect, appreciate or acknowledge me or my needs. Although I asked for nothing in return, one day I realized I've done a lot for others who don't even like me. So, I stopped.

And that's how I started making decisions moving forward, using the 'obligation' method. I would ask myself if replying to a message immediately felt like an obligation or something I wanted to do. If it felt like I was being guilt-tripped, pressured or manipulated to answer, I wouldn't until I felt it was the right time for me. Same with answering the phone, cooking dinner, or even choosing what conversations to engage in.

The simplest word was often the hardest to speak. No.

Finally, I considered myself first. If anything felt like an obligation, I wouldn't do it.

But I didn't have this mentality when I fell in love with my first boyfriend at age twelve. Over the years of our relationship, family members and acquaintances often asked why I was attracted to white boys but were never concerned with how that white boy and I treated each other.

Red flags were all over the relationship. Mixing alcohol, anger management issues, and a lack of proper communication skills, our teenage relationship evolved into us birthing two baby girls, dropping out of high school, and frequent domestic abuse.

I remember regaining consciousness on the couch with my tongue hanging from my mouth and his hands around my throat, and when he finally let me up, I looked to the couch across from us and straight into the scared eyes of my two baby girls as they watched and cried.

That is a lot for innocent babies to witness. And worse, I went on with life as if what they witnessed was normal.

And it was normal, normalized.

This was how most of the relationships around me looked, stemming all the way back to my childhood. This type of treatment in relationships was the norm.

And for that reason, I never thought to leave it. I told myself relationships were forever. I convinced myself that no matter what happened, if he didn't cheat on me then we could work it out.

So, he cheated but had the nerve to break up with me when I found the email from the girl who would be flying out to spend the week with him.

It wasn't until I expressed myself to a couple of close family members and broke down and cried that I realized how normalized abuse and cheating was in my family. As I explained how he hurt me, they didn't console me or reinforce that I would be better off on my own or with someone else, they told me that we "needed to stop playing and get back together."

With that, I attempted to suck the tears back into my eyes to prevent them from falling anymore. Why was I crying my heart out to people who refuse to acknowledge my pain? How could people who supposedly loved me encourage me to go back into a toxic relationship with the person who hurt me?

They must've believed I didn't deserve better, that I couldn't do better, that I wouldn't be better off on my own. Thankfully, I respected myself enough to recognize my worth and not allow anyone with that mindset to hold me back from the happiness, loyalty and security I deserved.

I knew then that I had to be my own cheerleader.

The apartment manager came by for overdue rent and when I told her my boyfriend broke up with me and left me for someone he barely met online, she gave me an unexpected solution: move out by the weekend and she wouldn't report it on my credit.

Karma works in mysterious ways.

So, with help from my sister who drove me to a nearby apartment complex, I found a small little studio apartment for me and my girls to move to. The small space was connected to a cramped kitchen where my babies sat on the floor in front of the oven to eat because of the lack of space for a dining table.

Little did I know, the Universe had stepped in and granted me a wish. The breakup was a blessing in disguise, and I often say it was the best thing that's ever happened to me because it led me to my current happy marriage.

I give full credit to my angels for bringing me and my husband together.

During my first relationship, I believed a real, loving partnership was one where there was no cheating or engaging in sex with anyone other than your partner. I thought loyalty and honesty were more valuable in a relationship than being respected, so I tolerated the verbal insults and violence. However, it took infidelity and him breaking up with me that made me realize the breakup was long overdue.

My angels saw that I was stuck in damaging chaos for far too long and intervened.

I rented a computer to begin writing my very first novel. Chat rooms were popular back in 2005, so I popped into one, and encountered the man who would become my current love of twenty years and counting.

At the time, I didn't know he would become my future husband and the man of my dreams. I never thought I could fall in love with someone online without even seeing them. Because our cell phones didn't have cameras and we didn't own webcams, after a couple months of endless phone calls and conversation, we ended up exchanging old high school pictures through email.

The next year, he moved to Arizona with only three-thousand dollars to his name and immediately became the father figure to two little girls at the age of twenty-one. I managed to get approved for a small, affordable two-bedroom apartment in the worst part of town to prepare for the adjustment.

We struggled financially for years, but improved bit by bit as time went on. I continued working in healthcare as a developmental care assistant for adults with disabilities. Although every two years I had to renew my CPR and First Aide certification, I refused to drive because I still didn't have a driver's license.

As his jobs evolved and his income improved, I began working solely for my younger sister who had cerebral palsy. She was bedridden, couldn't walk or talk, and was *supposedly* blind with the mentality of an infant. The most fun she had on her own was blowing raspberries or laughing at something near the ceiling only she could perceive. Mom would say the angels were talking to her.

With my husband earning his master's degree, his job changed, and his income increased, granting me the privilege to pursue my dream of writing full time.

I've been given everything I wished for: a loyal, handsome, sweet, honest, established, intelligent partner who gave me a third daughter and loves each of our kids as his own.

You're worthy of this. You were rewarded for learning and applying the many lessons you were given during your first relationship.

Is this why you intervened?

We intervened because you rejected the signs we sent you. All the red flags went unnoticed, and you needed to shift paths to get to where you are now.

Chapter 11

Hollywoodization

For the last few years, I've developed a habit of telling my husband how I feel while amongst people, from family members to complete strangers. For instance, while waiting inside the coffee shop for my iced white mocha, an unknown man walked in and waited in line to order.

Usually, I keep my head down to avoid direct eye contact, but I stole a few glances of the scenery while the man's back was turned to me. Although a good-looking young man, standing taller than the other customers, I sensed unease within his fake confidence. I detected his insecurity as he tugged his shirt a few times, adjusting how it rested on him. With his legs shoulder width apart, he centered his body weight and clasped his hands behind his back. Occasionally, he shifted his body from side to side, attempting to remain framed in the most flattering light.

Later, as me and my husband left the coffee shop, I told him, "That tall guy in line, did you see him? In the blue shirt?"

"Yeah. What about him?"

"He was nervous. Self-conscious about his looks but didn't want anyone to know."

My husband lifted an eyebrow. "How do you know?"

"I don't know." I shrugged as my rational brain suddenly reminded me there was no possible way I should know that without the guy telling me. "I guess I was reading his body language or something, but it feels like he was self-conscious about his clothes or how they fit or something. But he looked good. There's no reason he should feel that way. Just goes to show, even good-looking people sometimes think they're not good enough."

It comes to me like a knowing, a sureness, as if I was told directly from the person's mouth. But then my logical, rational human side chimes in to persuade me to find proof. And then I would wait for confirmation that I had been correct.

And then it occurred to me, what if this is what it's like to be "psychic"? What if the psychics we see on TV are sensationalized and it's not like seeing dead people and predicting the future. What if in the 3D world of science and the physical, being psychic is having the ability to read body language, facial expressions, and using your five senses to understand a person's state of being. What if those abilities were considered psychic insight or intuition?

Hollywood depicts psychics as outlandish, strange and speaking to beings that only they can see. They edit, script, and televise psychic mediums so they're depicted as crazy haired characters stopping passersby in grocery stores to give them messages from their recently deceased grandpa.

But what if real life mediumship is not so dramatic? What

if it's as subtle and mundane as sensing what the tall guy in the coffee shop line is thinking?

Most of us filter our desires and fantasies through one lens, the Hollywood brain, as we compare real life to the Hollywood lifestyle. A lot of people give up on their aspirations or refuse to even construct a dream because they feel it's out of reach. This is because we've Hollywoodized our goals. They see their dream as a Hollywood movie and expect the same results they often see onscreen.

But we all know, movies aren't real.

So, when the vision of our future matches a scene from a Hollywood blockbuster, it subconsciously leads us to believe our goals may be farfetched or unrealistic. The problem with that is we fail to see real life fulfillment as attainable.

For instance, one dream was to be financially stable to go on frequent trips with my husband, travel to different countries, experience new things, and rest and relax whenever we liked. Being happy and flourishing together.

For so long I strived for this life. Imagining looking out of the huge window of a lavish penthouse suite topping a multilevel building, while my tall, handsome husband wraps his arms around me from behind, kissing my neck he asks if I like the view as we smile and stare out at the late-night city lights. Like a scene from a steamy TV series or movie.

I only recently realized I've accomplished that goal years ago. I had been looking at my life as it played out, not realizing my reality matched the fantasy. The only thing separating my Hollywoodized goals from reality was the fancy edits and cut scenes. Me and my husband enjoyed the ability to experience Hollywood-like moments but with the inclusion of working hard to earn the money, arranging a sitter, scheduling the best times to call off work, booking plane tickets and hotel rooms, hunting down discounts and deals, and so on.

I already had what I wished for but was blinded by the Hollywoodized fantasy that I didn't realize was my reality.

Hollywood cuts out the filler, the mundane, the boring stuff from their movies. They don't waste time on characters doing redundant tasks, working exhausting hours, keeping up on hygiene, having boring conversations, or lying around scrolling through social media unless it's pivotal to the plot.

Hollywood depicts life as visually pleasing and cinematic. The actors, the set, the script are framed in a way to hook us and keep us engaged with every glamorized shot. Just like our imagination does with our desires, wishes and dreams.

If my life was Hollywoodized, it would be a rags to riches story. My character would be described as "the Black woman who came from a family with very little to end up with a big, two-story house in an upscale suburb." My Hollywoodized caricature would be like the Aunt Vivian of television sitcoms, the wealthy sibling, cousin or aunty with the "perfect" family. But in real life, I wasn't given luxuries or inherited money, I worked and fought for everything I earned. I came from nothing and trudged through many difficult lessons to be able to create my dream life. Those struggles are rarely depicted in movies or, if they are, they're mentioned in quick flashback scenes to be easily forgotten.

Once we strip down our goals to real world potential, we can see the possibilities within our reach. Expecting Hollywoodized results keeps us believing happily ever after is impossible. Once we shift our mindset to see real life without rose colored glasses, our goals and desires become attainable.

Having the dream life like our favorite celebrities may be

the goal for many, even as we fail to realize we've been persuaded by the lives of actors who live in the land of make believe.

We're often influenced by our favorite celebrities and what they promote, rarely realizing the business behind the screen. Our encounters with celebrities are through the media, be it social media, news media, internet, or so on.

What we see in a celebrity's life is what they choose to show us. We see their public persona that a team of public relations specialists, managers, lawyers, and the like put together. Their image is important because of their influence. They could sell products, change minds, influence behaviors and more.

The media acts as the barrier between the land of make believe and the real world to deliver those images and often sway public opinion on various issues, including our feelings on those celebrities.

These influences create trends that encourage the majority to follow. Before we know it, we act based on others actions due to wanting to be accepted or fit in, we follow without much thought. Not realizing less thinking and more following is herd mentality and often by design.

Those with influence are given influence like shepherds leading the sheep.

How do we break free?

Take off the mask. Be authentic. See through the Wizard of Oz veil and look behind the curtain. Understand how we're constantly being pulled back into the Hollywoodization mindset and fight the urge to follow.

Discover our true selves, embrace our uniqueness, believe in our power enough to exist without the mask. Doing so will help us set realistic goals and see where our lives have been Hollywoodized for the bad and the good.

Chapter 12

Understanding Why

I WAS TOLD MY father gave me my nickname because I liked crunchy foods. Noche rhymed with crunchy. And I would sway back and forth in my seat as I chomped on crunchy foods like fried chicken or potato chips, justifying the nickname.

Noche (No-Chee).

Only recently did I discover that rocking myself back and forth was self-soothing from undiagnosed generalized anxiety, along with thumb sucking which was a habit I was able to break in my early thirties. Even as a child, my family would try all sorts of tricks to prevent me from putting my thumb in my mouth, including smearing hot sauce on it. They tried everything short of therapy or medication. Afterall, I'm a Black female. So, my anxiety was considered "anger" and often presented itself as such.

Anger management classes did nothing to improve my condition, because anger wasn't the problem.

Noche grew up to be the fifteen-year-old thrust into motherhood. A young, pregnant black girl in poverty, dropping out of high school to raise a baby girl with her troubled teen boyfriend. What could go wrong?

Constantly in verbal arguments or physical fights with my siblings or mother, I always felt attacked and on the lonely side of the aisle, even when what I fought for was right, just, or true.

My hard work and talents went unnoticed or often downplayed. Support was hard to come by.

As time went on, Noche held onto the belief that blood was thicker than water. Family get-togethers with the siblings and their kids were routine events. It was expected to be involved with holidays or birthday plans or celebrations even if attending was later met with regret. If the event concluded with no one angry or little drama, that would be considered a rare success. Usually, details of the event would make its rounds, focusing on everything but what went right.

Noche would have a hard time saying *no*, wanting to help and be of aid. Something I learned in the healthcare field, as a medical assistant volunteering at a local hospital. For income, I was a home health aide helping disabled adults cook, clean, and bathe. I changed adult diapers and wiped ass because it felt good to bring relief to others. Noche gave her time, money, energy, expertise and advice to anyone who asked without question.

Noche was overly generous. Offering rides, paying for meals, planning events, donating to funerals, fitting the restaurant bill, giving expensive gifts, paying for others' bills, providing tarot readings, offering advice, giving away free books, being a listening ear, providing a place to stay, and so much more. Even when those who benefited never showed up, changed plans last minute, lied, refused to attend my parties or even my wedding, took advantage of me, used me, and refused to reciprocate.

Noche tried to be the bigger person in every situation, looking at people's potential instead of their actions which always spoke louder than words.

When I announced my novel got attention from Hollywood executives, I pretended not see the disinterested looks and the lack of engagement from those who I expected to be thrilled. I wrote that book to cope with the passing of my younger brother and sister and thought those who loved them too would be proud. However, when around those closest to me, Noche pretended the accomplishment wasn't a big deal because that's how others treated it.

Noche always dimmed her light in her family's presence, never boasting about her achievements or successes because family and friends were struggling. So, I learned to find something to complain about too.

However, by the turn of the new year 2025, when Pluto entered Aquarius, Leslie said enough is enough. Life needed to shift and so did I. I got serious and went deep. Stepping back from what drained me, I put up boundaries. And through a year of intense introspection and self-reflection, I found my voice and discovered my power.

The word *no* is now a full sentence. Period.

Self-care is now a priority.

Honesty and authenticity are now a requirement.

I see the truth behind the lack of support within my circle.

In fact, I no longer have a circle. I've fully come to terms with the fact that my light is too powerful to dim for anyone. I say what I want and mean what I say. I celebrate my successes loud, proud and unapologetically. I know what I'm capable of and don't need anyone to validate me or my talents.

If someone doesn't like me that's their right, but their dislike won't stop my light from shining.

I left Noche and what she represents with those who refused to see me as anything more. And not many are welcomed to come with me where I'm heading in my desired life.

When I say I will do something, I get it done because I keep my promises, especially the vows to myself. How can I expect others to treat me with value if I don't honor my own worth?

Once I make a decision, I set out to accomplish it.

If you cheat on me, I'm out.

I'm going to be a respected writer.

No matter what, my kids come first.

Stop wasting time on things that do not serve my best interest.

Remove unhealthy relationships from my life.

Which leads me here in solitude away from the distractions to create my happiest timeline. In my solitude I found clarity and realized just how little others valued me. I set boundaries and those boundaries came with clear and abrupt distance for *my* wellbeing and growth.

This shift is like a ship ready to set sail and explore the furthest reaches of sea, yet an anchor is clawing at the ocean bottom, holding it back. The anchor represents people who don't believe in two-sided relationships, who diminish our accomplishments, who secretly hate to see us succeed or get ahead. Setting my boundary was me severing the chain that connected my ship to the anchor, so I can finally set off on my voyage.

I had an epiphany that I was meant to write this book, and after finally coming to terms with that, I kept quiet. No one knows I'm writing this book. Not my husband or my three girls, and they see me every day. They all know I'm writing a book, but they have no idea its subject matter. I call it my "secret project."

I'm still working on my "being seen" era. I'm still vulnerable to others' opinions, and don't want anyone to influence this book or sway me to not publish it. And that message was given to me by my angels through tarot, while I worked through that growth.

So much insight comes from online pick-a-card tarot readings. Whenever I choose a card, its message highly resonates. I've had a business giving these types of tarot readings online for four years. Although I no longer read as a service, I still pull cards for my girls and myself to this day. I taught myself to read them, practicing spiritual work like meditation, journaling, and studying each card until I was ready to "give intuitive advice to empower your life."

Watching tarot readings from a diverse selection of readers is a regular routine. Many of the messages confirmed the same thing:

You will use your talent to co-create with your guides to manifest a book that you will share with the world. Keep this close to your heart until you finish writing it. It will be a tough climb, but you will reap the benefit of awakening others to their power within. Every resource you need to

complete this soul mission will be provided. Don't worry. You are on the right path.

After a long time and a lot of convincing, I tuned in to my heart and listened.

Just the last few months I've been going through what is known as a Dark Night of the Soul, where I had to face my shadows to understand my ego or the 3D human side of me. I had to come to terms with deep-seated issues, learn to communicate better, set boundaries, practice self-care, take breaks, work at my own pace, stop comparing myself to others, find my voice, freely express myself and become fully authentic.

To get to the place I needed to be to write this book and have the experience to call myself a master of my craft, required all the things that happened in my life to take place. I had to learn from each lesson, grow, change, and become enlightened enough to be in this position.

My higher self, that powerful inner soul, helped draw the blueprints while my human navigated this physical world to grow enough to discover that soul and her power within.

As of the year 2025, Earth's energies are fully polarized. There is an ultimate split occurring, where many will have to choose where they stand. There are two sides, the good side and its opposite. Many creatives will be called to remove their masks and be seen and heard, using their creativity as their weapon of choice.

I was guided by my angels and guides, and now my human and my higher self are integrated and working to accomplish the same goal for the good of humanity.

Earlier I feared evil had won, but it has not. Just like the land of make-believe, things just aren't as they seem.

I imagine a scene in my mind's eye: My higher self, clad in armor, sword in hand at the edge of an overcast battlefield. The eyes of the opposition zero in on me. As they charge, upon the swing of my blade, heads roll.

That same power lives inside us all.

⬦

Tarot readings play on TV as background noise while I'm writing this, and I instantly receive a message:

You're writing a book about your destiny.

Warmth floods my heart space like a growing fire bubbling up inside my throat.

Is that why my heart hurts, because this is true? My higher self if glowing to let me know we're in sync?

Or maybe it's heartburn.

I couldn't contain my laughter as I sense both sides of me agree.

At night, I'm able to relax in my solitude and peace. Usually everyone is asleep or tucked away in their corner of the house. This is when most of my spiritual messages are communicated, spoken through random online tarot readings, specifically answering my questions. In this solitude, I can finally hear my higher self and guides as rapid thoughts and clear authority in my mind. When a message is on point, my heart aches. A similar feeling to falling in love.

You forget very easily. Sometimes you forget we even had conversations.

They were right. Because as soon as I wake up in the mornings, most of what I had channeled, gained, or experienced the night before was forgotten. Or I would question or doubt it until I find peace again the next night. Even still, I'd have a flash of divine inspiration with details and all and must be reminded by Spirit that I should write it down immediately before I forget it.

That's the battle between my body and my spirit. My logical mind tries to make sense of everything and find solid proof. It sticks to the facts and science and sees the world through those eyes. While my higher self, my soul and power within, continually makes herself known while providing insight and direction through unconventional means like physical sensation, intense thoughts that feel true or like a knowing, repeated numbers like 1212, and signs and synchronicities.

No. I am no different than anyone else. If every person on this earth are the fingers of Source, we're as different and special as its fingerprints. Everyone has flaws. No one is perfect. This is the nature of the human being.

However, I always viewed my fingerprint as unique. It is, isn't it?

We're unique individuals connected to one source.

As a child, one of my teachers asked the students a series of questions and instructed us to write down our answers.

"Think about your favorite color? Why do you like it so much?"

I thought about it for a second, jotting down the answer almost immediately. "Purple. Because it's different and unique."

"Your favorite color represents you and what you said about that color represents how you see yourself."

Ever since, I've described myself as unique and I lived by that trait. I embody the definition of that word in everything I create, be it with my singing or music, my oil paintings, or my creative writings. Being unique, different, and one of a kind empowered me. It fueled my imagination, creativity, and self-expression.

Every story I write must be different from others in its category. If it's too mainstream, I try to find a way to make it my own even if it means not following formulas, tropes and convention. Those times I followed the conventional, mainstream and its rules, I ended up burning myself out at 150k words and unhappy with my lack of motivation to create. Following trends, tropes and formulas, writing to the market, being mainstream bores me to my core because it's not what I came here to do.

We're more powerful than that.

There are millions of unique individuals around the world who will tap into their unique talents, abilities, and gifts with authenticity to help remind people that they have a power inside of themselves as well.

I know I'm one of them. I am fortunate to be fully aware of my physical side as well as my spiritual side. And although everyone has these sides, if they believe it or not, being able to combine the two has given me insight I would have never known otherwise.

My spirit and my physical self are now integrated, allowing me to live as my powerful inner spirit. Now as I walk the earth, what I truly feel inside will be reflected on the outside.

In many ways, I believe this is why my husband was sent to me. Although he is a skeptic, his logical, scientific brain keeps my logical side engaged and stimulated. In fact, his skepticism led me to question organized religion. After years of analyzing the contradictions, harm, hypocrisy and intolerance that was often practiced and preached in these institutions, I've come to understand organized religion to act as a business, using the same dysfunctional system as governments, militaries, the media and other groups that profit from and impose excessive control over others through fear.

He also respectfully entertains my spiritual side and often engages in spiritual discussions with me, keeping my psychic mind stimulated and engaged.

On a late evening run to the coffee shop, deep in discussion I looked at him as he pulled into the drive through. Before we approached the speaker, I ended our lengthy conversation about being progressive with, "Yes, I'm an empath who respects all living things in nature and hug trees. That's who I am, purple hair and all. I'm proud of that."

Being progressive as well but not as obsessed with nature as I am, he chuckled and nodded in agreement before placing our orders.

Once ordered, we pulled around the corner as the cashier poked her head out of the window, revealing vibrant purple hair. She greeted us, took our payment, and turned to get our drinks.

"See?" I took the opportunity to secretly gesture to her.

"That was synchronicity. That's the Universe confirming we are on the right track."

He nodded and began to fidget with something on the console. "Yea. She has purple hair," he acknowledged.

"Listen." I turned in my seat to catch his attention. "Like I said, this is who I am. So, you're gonna have to get used to this. You know?" I teased.

"Now *you* listen." He mirrored me and shifted in his seat. "I've loved you for over twenty years now. And as much as you talk about your angels, get excited over repeated numbers, and befriend crows… If I didn't run then, I'm not running now or ever."

Every day I thank my angels for him.

I appreciate my spirit guides and angels since the beginning because they repeatedly show they exist and are guiding me. They helped me remember my power and purpose and urge me to embrace change. They remind me that I co-create the life I want to live and the world I want to live in. They show me what I came to do and are with me now as I do it.

Little does my husband know, I call him my spiritual confidant. Although he is a skeptic, he has never judged me or my views, and therefore I confide in him. He knows more about my spiritual side than anyone else in my life. I explain a lot of spiritual concepts to him, but many times I often discover spiritual gifts, epiphanies and perceptions during our late-night drives and discussions.

I sense in him that at times he thinks I'm extremely eccentric or odd yet innocent and passionate about my beliefs, even if he doesn't fully understand it. I've come to accept that because I know my husband's inner spiritual power anticipates the moment he's discovered.

I appreciate the human gifts I was given, to write, to sing, to craft, to create. And I appreciate the spiritual gifts I was also given, to read people, to communicate with Spirit through intuition and channeling, to understand spiritual language, and to act as inspiration to others.

Like everyone else, I will always have my flaws and make mistakes. I learn from every mistake even if it takes repeating it a few times to learn and grow. I treat life like trying to master a skill, the more you practice and apply what you've learned, the better you become. The music we make will be dissonant and off key at the start. That's because we have no idea what we're doing, but as we keep playing, learning as we go, avoiding the same mistakes, we get better. We advance.

And when you play fair with others and treat them well, the music we create together harmonizes and becomes a beautiful symphony.

If my life were a story, like biblical parables or Mama's tales, I would hope the details of my testimony connect to those who hear it and inspire them to seek their inner power to positively shift not only their life but the world.

We must realize we're a band of people on Earth with a spirit inside of us that's trying to ace the exam we call Life. Our spiritual mentors, our guides, are trying to get us through it the most effective way possible.

The only question is…are you ready to listen?

THE END

CHANNELED AFFIRMATIONS
JUST FOR YOU

Analyzing my past allows me to understand who
I am and discover my authentic self, but my past
does not define me. I decide who I am today and
who I choose to show up as in my future.

I create the life I want to live through my actions. What I
put out into the world finds its way back to me. My power
is strong enough to not only alter my life but humanity.

I am ready to co-create with the Universe, to shift
the scales of life toward positivity, light, and love.

I identify the masks I fabricated and strip back each
layer to reveal my true, authentic self without fear.

I listen to my intuition and follow my heart
to lead me down the right path toward
abundance, prosperity and success.

I no longer fear life's lessons because they shape
me into the strongest version of myself.

I accept all that's on my path ahead
because it is designed for me by me.

I, _____ claim this message.

About the Author

Leslie Lee Sanders launched her writing career in 2005, publishing over thirty books across multiple genres. Writing as **L.L. Sanders**, she crafts psychological thrillers and horror, while her works under **Leslie Lee Sanders** explore diverse romance and dystopian fiction, often blending genres in unexpected ways.

In 2025, Leslie published a first in nonfiction, a deeply personal spiritual self-help memoir she hopes will inspire others to find their power and manifest the life they desire, titled *Ready to Listen?*

You can find more about Leslie and her books on her website: *http://www.llsanders.com*

You can write to Leslie at:

Lls4sanders@gmail.com